THE
LANDSCAPED
ROCK AND WATER
GARDEN

THE LANDSCAPED ROCK AND WATER GARDEN

By

FRANK W. ORME

(Drawings by the author)

NIMROD PRESS LTD
P.O. Box 1
Liss, Hants, GU33 7PR
England

ISBN 1 85259 006 5

Printed & bound by
R J Acford Chichester
Sussex

Publisher:
NIMROD PRESS LTD
P.O. Box 1
Liss, Hants
England

CONTENTS

LIST OF ILLUSTRATIONS

ACKNOWLEDGEMENTS

The author wished to place on record his appreciation of the advice and assistance received from many sources, which greatly eased the task of preparing this book. Particular mention must be made of the following, who supplied illustrations and gave unreserved permission for them to be reproduced herein — coupled with the generous offer of assistance if required — to each I tender my thanks:

Stapeley Water Gardens Ltd. 92 London Road, Stapeley, Nantwich, Cheshire CW5 7JL.

Hozelock Ltd., Haddenham, Aylesbury, Buckinghamshire HP17 9JD.

Stuart Turner Ltd, Engineers, Henley-on-Thames, Oxfordshire RG9 2AD.

PREFACE

Water has long found a place in the garden, for there is a magical charm about water that beckons all to gaze into its depth. No matter one's age, few can resist the temptation to pause beside a rippling stream or stare into the underwater world of a placid pool. From time immemorial, water has exercised an enchantment for man and will, no doubt, continue to do so for years to come.

Far back in history, long before the birth of Christ, there is evidence of artificial pools being combined with gardens. It is more than likely that those early pools were designed more for utilitarian purposes, rather than ornamental, where live fish could be kept until required for culinary use. Even so, there can be little doubt that the pools were also found attractive, for in the tombs of the Egyptian rulers of those times there are reliefs which depict fish in pools; the lotus is also figured on many of the monuments.

During the campaigns of Alexander the Great, (356-323 B.C.) the Greeks made contact with Asia and discovered a geat deal about the gardens and plants of that area. Theophrastus, the so-called father of botany, recorded much of the information gathered by the wisemen who travelled with Alexander, and so helped to spread the knowledge further afield.

It is known that the Romans developed the art of gardening, for Pliny, the naturalist, (23-79 A.D.) made mention of them in his writings. However, his nephew, Pliny the younger, (61-c. 113 A.D.) provided a much greater source of information about the Roman gardens, in his many letters. Indeed, contemporary literature contains many references to the fishpools in the country villas of ancient Rome, where the keeping of fish for ornamental purposes was very popular. Archaeological excavations have revealed that the gardens of rich Romans contained, in almost every instance, a fish pool with marble fountains.

There was a period during which Persian gardens reached a high standard and were greatly admired. Victoria Sackville-West, when describing the garden of Madrasah at Isfahan, wrote of the long range of blue-tiled buildings, and a long pool in which they were reflected; also of the purple lilac and the irises.

India, too, had its water gardens where the central canal was a particular feature of the design. The Taj Mahal, built circa 1650, is an outstanding example.

In the oriental gardens and parks the ornamental fish pool has, for many centuries, been a notable feature, the house, garden and pool being treated in such a way as to form a harmonious whole.

The Chinese have long been famous for their ornamental fish pools. Marco Polo wrote of them when describing his travels (1271-95). Although not large, many had several small pools set in masses of rock, arranged to resemble miniature mountains. Miniature trees, stunted in proportion to the rockwork, set here and there, were grown in concealed earthenware containers. Bamboos, azaleas and hydrangeas all added their charm to the scene.

Japanese ornamental fish pools and gardens have enjoyed fame for a great number of years, for water forms an almost indispensable part of virtually all gardens in Japan, from the large public park down to the miniature bowl-garden. When water is not available, sand is skilfully employed to create the illusion of a stream, and rocks are used to simulate waterfalls. The art of designing this dry landscape is nearly always so perfect that the illusion is complete. These gardeners take great care to ensure harmony and, whilst the pools may vary in shape, the water is kept perfectly clear. Everything is so arranged that the finished garden appears to have existed for centuries.

Alhambra, the famous Moresco-Spanish palace which overlooks the river Darro, was begun by Mahomed I (1232-72) and completed during the reign of Yusuf I (1333-54). The most splendid of the remaining parts — are the Court of the Lions, so called from the twelve marble lions grouped around a centre fountain and basin; the Court of the Fishpond, which has a length of 150 feet (45.720 metres) and is completely filled by a marble pool.

Spanish gardens are well known for their water features. The palace gardens at Aranjuez, near Madrid, contain fish pools and a number of fountains. At Seville, in the gardens of the Alcazar, the fountains were cunningly designed to give unsuspecting visitors a surprise cold shower.

In Italy, the Renaissance brought about a remarkable improvement in the development of garden design, many being truly magnificent in both concept and design-layout, with ingenious fountains and terraces and superb statuary. The fish pool was an essential feature in the design of every garden of any size. It is the wide avenues, pools and fountains which form the main features in gardens of the period.

Buontalenti designed the garden of the Villa Pratolino, at Florence, for Francesco de' Medici (the Bastard of Cosimo). This contained its share of water, as did Villa Aldobrandini, (at Frascati), which is noted for its fountains and pools.

During the Renaissance many of the great artists — such as Raphael — were commissioned by the wealthy land-owners to design the elegant fountains and pools that graced their gardens. The greatest heights were reached in the design of the gardens at Villa d'Este, at Tivoli, where water dominates. The designer, Pirro Ligori, made use of water in every possible manner and created a truly remarkable landscape.

As the style spread progressively northwards, its movement had an impact in England, and this resulted in Cardinal Wolsey creating the first of the 'grand-scale' gardens at Hampton Court. The Tudor nobility became so enraptured that the style was quickly embraced. Large and small gardens were adorned with close-clipped topiary, elaborate fountains and pools. The flower beds were set in geometrical patterns known as 'knots', with grassed or paved paths and carefully-sited seats.

As the influence of the Renaissance period passed it was noticeable that the French gardens became even grander in their scale. The style was architectural and formal in design, requiring that the garden should be walled and have elaborately-designed flower beds, together with clipped evergreens. Spreading far afield, the style reached British shores during 1660, at the time of the Restoration.

In France, Louis XIV began construction of the palace of Versailles in 1661. The gardens, designed by Le Nôtre, still reveal much of its departed glory, being laid out with imposing pools and fountains. Fontainebleau is also famed for its water features. In England, at about the same time, the well-known Blenheim Palace was being built. The 2,500 acre (1011.75 hectare) park is thought to have been designed by Sir John Vanburgh, and contains a large lake within its scheme. Frederick the Great died in 1786 at Sanssouci, a palace which he had constructed on the outskirts of Potsdam, near Berlin. The rococo decorations, parks and fountains still remain one of the great attractions for visitors to the town.

The French style, with its adherence to regularity, symmetry and contrived art, did not remain in favour with the English and the 18th Century witnessed a revolution in the design of English gardens. As a result of the calculated planning and guidance of such masters as Lancelot 'Capability' Brown (1715-83) the severity and rigour of the formal garden came to an end; straight paths and avenues were eliminated as nature and irregularity took over. Under 'Capability' Brown, who had a preference for following nature in the planning of gardens, the true landscaped garden began. Gone were the long, straight, water-filled canals of former times; in their place were artifially-created serpentined lakes. The surrounding land was skilfully landscaped, with great care, into a contrived but controlled naturalness. The natural design of Nature had become the key to good garden design. Outstanding examples of this art can be seen at Chatsworth and Trentham and, of course, Woburn Abbey is famous for its pools.

With the industrial growth of the 19th Century, and the accompanying urbanisation of nearby land, many more people, income permitting, were able to enjoy the pursuit of gardening. This brought about a corresponding increase in public interest in the quest for horticultural knowledge. In the main, gardens were much smaller in scale, for the grandiose schemes of other years were no longer possible, and this compelled the gardener to take great care in the planning to ensure that the most effective use was made of the available land.

The Second World War accelerated many changes and, in its aftermath, it was found that maintaining very large, park-like gardens often proved economically impossible for their owners. With a few notable exceptions, the death-knell had been sounded for the large estates and many were sold. Once — large ornamental gardens disappeared under the onslaught of the bulldozer, to be replaced by the bricks and mortar of new housing estates. Such re-development resulted in the creation of a vast number of small garden plots, which, of necessity, did not allow the scope in design of earlier days.

Not only have gardens changed over the years, but the people who tend them have also changed. In those days of yesteryear landowners employed a number of professional gardeners to attend to the many essential tasks that are necessary to maintain a garden in first-class condition. Each of those professional gardeners had spent some time, as apprentices or such, in learning the skills of their chosen craft. The majority of today's gardeners are in the main, amateurs who, whilst earning their living in other spheres, look upon gardening as a pleasantly relaxing hobby. As the number of small gardens multiplied, so more unskilled people began to look after their own plots of land and by trial and error, very often turned them into attractive little havens of colour.

In order to satisfy the public's thirst for knowledge and guidance, a great many informative books have been written on the subject of gardening over the years. These books range from the very simple to works of great expertise. There are those which deal with the basic 'A.B.C.' of gardening, whilst others are very specialised, in that they deal with one specific aspect, be it a group of plants, a method or branch of gardening, and such like. There is hardly any limit to the choice, and most interests are catered for.

The author of this present book has not set out to compete with other gardening books — it is, after all, a subject which has been well covered by others. However, he does feel that there can be few gardens that would not be greatly enhanced by the inclusion of some water feature. The ornamental fish pool may be smaller than of old, and its surroundings less imposing, yet the modern water garden is none the worse for that — irrespective of how large or small, all water has an attraction peculiar to itself. It therefore seems logical to combine the attractions of the water garden with those of the terrestrial garden, to form a garden which contains the charms of both.

Few hard and fast rules have been laid down; rather an attempt has been made to guide the reader, although some rules must be obeyed, especially where the health of fish is concerned, and to this end some pages have been devoted to their care.

No two gardens are ever identical, nor should they be, for each is a reflection of its creator's personal design and endeavour. It is sincerely hoped that the following pages will serve to point the reader along the correct paths, and so ensure that any venture into the various types of water gardening, and the accompanying landscape, will produce a scene that others can only admire and, perhaps, secretly envy.

If those garden designers of old could recognise the attractions of employing water within their garden schemes, why not the modern gardener? Throughout the history of gardening water has often been incorporated into the garden design, in one form or another, for nothing has more attraction that the placid face of the well-planned pool, or the sound of a rippling stream on a warm summer day. It beckons from afar, and invites one to linger in contemplation of the languidly swimming fish as they glide beneath the leaves of the majestic water-lillies. Fountains, canals, pools and lakes — they have all, at one time or another, found their place in the garden design — for the shape in which water is employed is limitless in form, and nearly always adds beauty to the scene.

That which was achieved on the grand scale, in days long past, can often be successfully imitated — albeit on a much reduced scale — by the present-day gardener, in the much smaller area of the modern garden plot. Possibly many people are put off the idea of water gardening because they suspect that they are a particularly costly feature, both in time and money. This belief is far from the truth for, in terms of labour, water gardens are the least demanding of all, and even the loveliest garden will be transformed by adding a rock garden and pool.

Water is always fascinating. Surrounded by rocks and plants it can become an area of great beauty, a place of peace and serenity. A formal pool, set in a paved patio, can add tranquil charm to an evening meal outdoors. Whether the area be large or small the possibilities are endless, and water will bring a magical life of its own — an irresistable attraction to all age groups.

ILLUSTRATIONS
IN
COLOUR

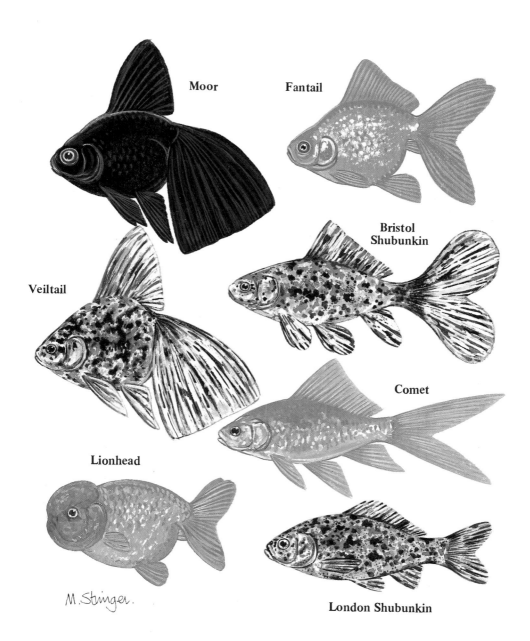

Moor

Fantail

Bristol
Shubunkin

Veiltail

Comet

Lionhead

M. Stringer.

London Shubunkin

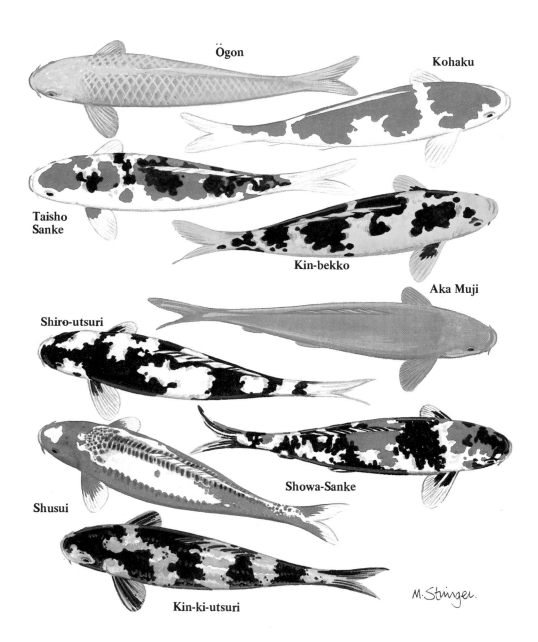

Ögon

Kohaku

Taisho
Sanke

Kin-bekko

Aka Muji

Shiro-utsuri

Showa-Sanke

Shusui

Kin-ki-utsuri

M. Stringer.

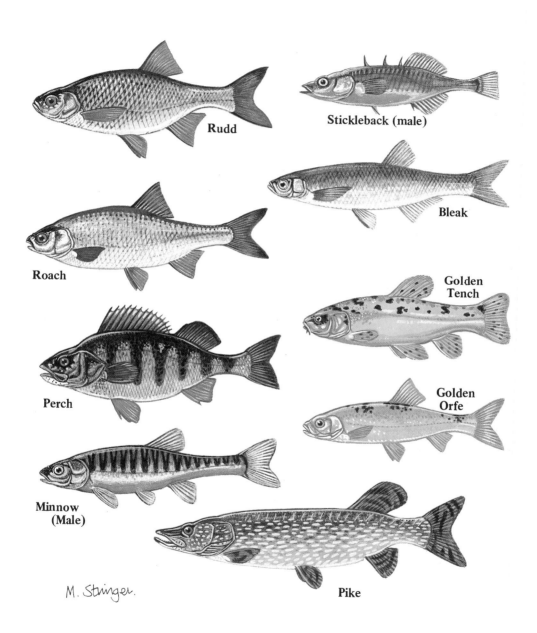

Rudd

Stickleback (male)

Bleak

Roach

Golden
Tench

Perch

Golden
Orfe

Minnow
(Male)

M. Stringer.

Pike

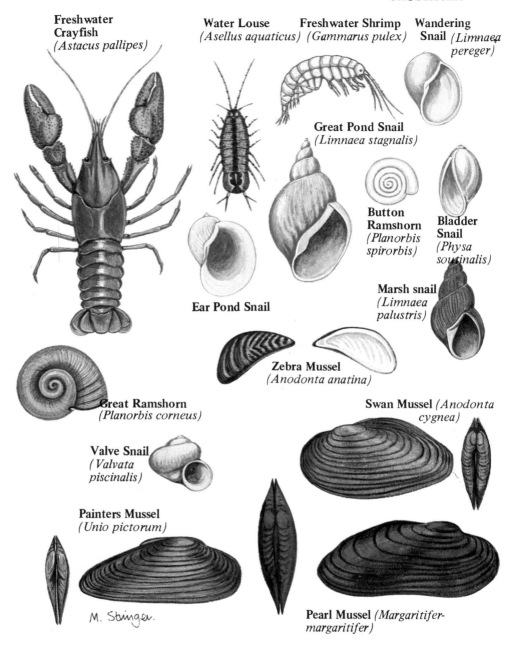

Freshwater Crayfish *(Astacus pallipes)*

Water Louse *(Asellus aquaticus)*

Freshwater Shrimp *(Gammarus pulex)*

Wandering Snail *(Limnaea pereger)*

Great Pond Snail *(Limnaea stagnalis)*

Button Ramshorn *(Planorbis spirorbis)*

Bladder Snail *(Physa soutinalis)*

Ear Pond Snail

Marsh snail *(Limnaea palustris)*

Zebra Mussel *(Anodonta anatina)*

Great Ramshorn *(Planorbis corneus)*

Swan Mussel *(Anodonta cygnea)*

Valve Snail *(Valvata piscinalis)*

Painters Mussel *(Unio pictorum)*

M. Stringer.

Pearl Mussel *(Margaritifer-margaritifer)*

FROGS and TOADS (Showing Stages of Development)

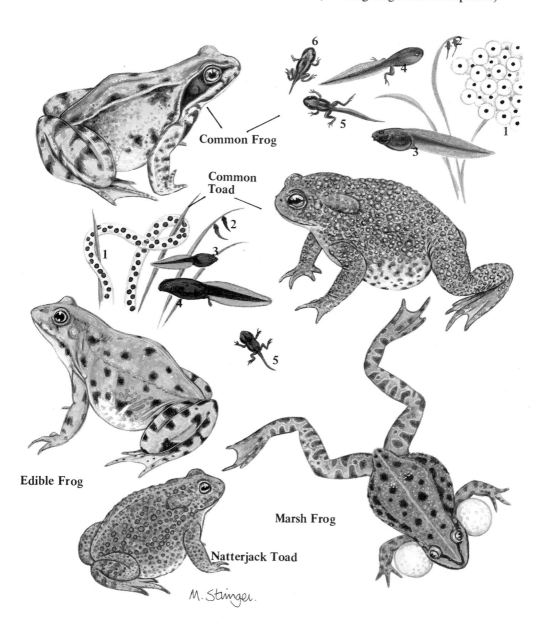

Common Frog

Common Toad

Edible Frog

Natterjack Toad

Marsh Frog

M. Stringer.

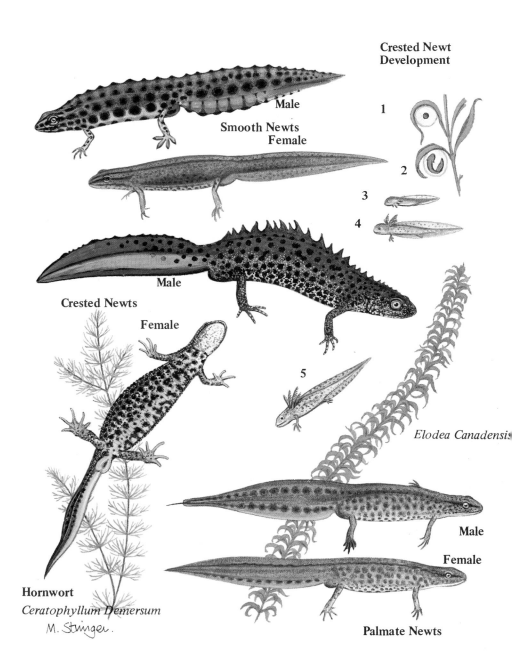

Crested Newt
Development

Male

Smooth Newts
Female

1

2

3

4

Male

Crested Newts

Female

5

Elodea Canadensis

Male

Female

Hornwort
Ceratophyllum Demersum
M. Stringer.

Palmate Newts

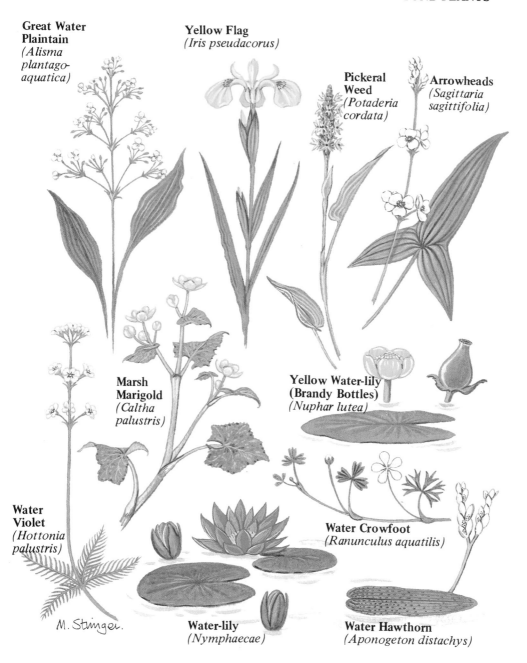

Great Water Plaintain
(Alisma plantago-aquatica)

Yellow Flag
(Iris pseudacorus)

Pickeral Weed
(Potaderia cordata)

Arrowheads
(Sagittaria sagittifolia)

Marsh Marigold
(Caltha palustris)

Yellow Water-lily (Brandy Bottles)
(Nuphar lutea)

Water Violet
(Hottonia palustris)

Water Crowfoot
(Ranunculus aquatilis)

M. Stringer.

Water-lily
(Nymphaecae)

Water Hawthorn
(Aponogeton distachys)

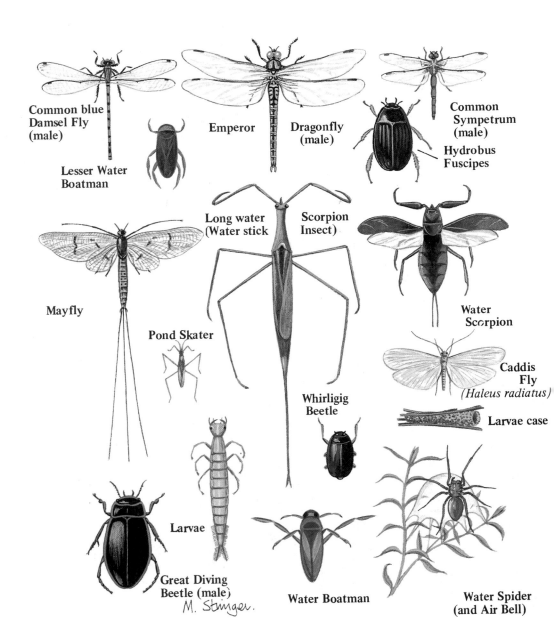

Common blue
Damsel Fly
(male)

Emperor

Dragonfly
(male)

Common
Sympetrum
(male)

Lesser Water
Boatman

Hydrobus
Fuscipes

Long water
(Water stick

Scorpion
Insect)

Mayfly

Water
Scorpion

Pond Skater

Caddis
Fly
(Haleus radiatus)

Whirligig
Beetle

Larvae case

Larvae

Great Diving
Beetle (male)
M. Stinger.

Water Boatman

Water Spider
(and Air Bell)

Chapter 1

SITE PREPARATION

The dictionary defines 'landscape' as 'a picture representing country scenery'. More particularly, the definition of landscape-gardening
is given as 'the art of laying out grounds so as to develop their natural
beauties'. Before any attempt is made to follow either of these pre-
cepts, it is, quite obviously, necessary to look at the site of the
intended garden.

First let us consider a plot of land adjoining a newly built residence
— such as can be found in large numbers on new housing estates —
which may well contain various builders rubble. Often the contractor
will have spread a thin surface of top-soil over the site, however, this
is purely a cosmetic treatment and little more.

TRENCHING THE SITE

In order to remove all unwanted material and prepare the ground
for future operations, it is essential that it be deeply dug. The correct
method is known as **double digging** or **bastard trenching,** and is the
best and most common way of dealing with soil in most cases. It is
called double digging because two layers of soil are broken up during
the process. Although two layers are broken, they remain at their
original level — in other words the sub-soil remains on the bottom
to be covered by the upper level of top soil.

Commence by digging a trench across one end of the plot. The
trench should be deep as the blade of the spade, and about 15 in.
(381mm) wide. The soil should be removed to the other end of the
plot, where it will remain until the digging is completed. The base of
the trench should then be dug-over with a large digging-fork, to break
up the soil to at least the depth of the fork-prongs. Any turf or other
vegetable matter can be buried in this lower layer of broken soil. It
is advisable to turn the turf over, so that it is buried upside down.
Next, turn the following 15 in. of top soil over into the trench, leaving
a second trench of similar width and depth. Repeat this process until
the opposite end of the plot is reached, filling in the final trench with
the soil removed from the first trench.

1

If it is found, as may be the case, that the dark, fertile soil has been buried by the builder, this should be brought to the surface. The easiest way is to open out a very wide trench, in the same way as is done for bastard trenching. Make the trench about 30 in. (762mm) wide, to a depth of one spit — the depth of the spade blade — then take out a further trench 15 in. (381mm) wide and one spit deep. Keep the fertile soil in one heap and the sub-soil in another. Now turn the poor soil from the next 15 inches into the deep section of the first trench. Then turn the second width of sub-soil on to the top of this first trench. This will create a second trench, which is two spits deep in the first half, and one spit deep in the second half. Continue in this fashion over the whole plot, so that eventually the poor, sticky soil is buried beneath the original dark, fertile soil.

During the process of trenching, all rubble and unwanted material should be removed. Later it may be possible to bury much of it in a low part of the garden, to form drainage to a potentially wet spot.

Ideally this preparatory work should be carried out during the autumn. The ground can then be left rough over the winter months, during which it will settle and frost will break up the clods of soil. Lime can be spread over the surface to be washed in by the rains. As lime has the effect of breaking up large lumps of stiff soil, the combined effects of this and the frost will make the ground much easier to work in the following spring, instead of it being hard and lumpy.

CORRECT USE OF THE SPADE

Digging is one of the most important of the gardening operations. An experienced gardener can dig much faster and certainly much more easily than the novice. Most beginners end a day of digging by complaining of aches and pains, and have blistered hands as their reward. These problems are usually due to the incorrect use of tools rather than the work itself. As with all other tools, the spade should be kept in a clean, bright, sharp condition; a dull, rusty spade is a most inefficient tool.

The correct way for most people to hold the spade is to have the right hand on top of the handle, and the left hand about half-way down the shaft. The spade is lifted and then driven downwards so that the blade cuts vertically into the ground. The blade should penetrate to its full depth, and this will probably require some assistance from the foot. When the blade has entered the soil, the spade should be levered backwards and forwards to loosen a cube of the solid soil, which is then lifted on the spade, and turned completely over. If the spade is driven into the ground at an angle, instead of vertically, it does not give such deep penetration, nor does it cut a clean-sided trench.

PREPARING AN EXISTING GARDEN

Where the garden is already established, and perhaps neglected and overgrown, it will be necessary to decide what, if anything, is to be retained. Possibly there is an existing rockery which is poorly constructed and/or badly sited, but has re-usable stone, which can be placed out of the way until required. Unsightly paths can be broken up, perhaps to be utilized in an area of crazy paving. Old, worn-out shrubs and such like should be taken up and burnt, or otherwise disposed of. Any plant, rose or shrub which is to be retained for future use can be heeled, as a temporary measure, into the soil in an out of the way spot. This is accomplished by digging a shallow trench, the base of which is lightly broken up with a fork and then well watered. The plant is also given a good soaking with water. Then, with a fork, the roots are carefully loosened from the surrounding soil before being transferred to the trench. When all of the transfers have been made, the roots should be covered with soil, which is then firmed with the foot. Finally, the trench is again given a good watering. This operation is best carried out during the autumn, when most subjects are dormant. At other times care should be taken to see that the trench does not dry out too much. Even so, there may be some losses.

Little can be done to improve an impoverished, weed-filled lawn. In the long-term it will pay dividends to skim off the old turf and start again. The turves can be stacked, upside down, until they can be buried during the course of digging.

Having cleared the area of all unwanted material, the ground should be thoroughly bastard trenched, as described earlier in this chapter. During this operation all weeds, roots, etcetera should be removed for burning; this is essential if future weed problems are to be avoided as far as possible.

With the completed clearance, and thorough digging, of the site, the area can be left to settle down in preparation for the desired landscaping, which may include some alteration of the existing levels in order to contour the surface into shallow banks and valleys. Such contouring will give a naturalness to the finished garden that would be difficult to achieve if the area were completely flat, like a billiard table.

NATURE OF SOIL

Before leaving this chapter it may be worthwhile to consider the nature of soil, for soil is not dead matter. It is full of living bacteria which needs air and moisture in order to perform their duties. Air and moisture in the soil depend as much on its texture as on any chemical additions that might be made, and the improvement of the texture is the essential first step in cultivation.

Soils are composed of varying proportions of sand, chalk, clay, gravel and humus (decaying animal and vegetable matter.) The various types of soil are called by different names, according to which of the ingredients predominates.

Sand is made up of grains of quartz and other rocks (mainly silica) together with mineral impurities. Sandy soils are *light* soils, and they may contain a small amount of plant food.

Clay consists of similar material, but ground to a much finer texture and bound together with a sticky material which is actually a compound of silica, aluminia, and water. *Heavy,* or *stiff* soil, is a soil which contains a very large proportion of clay.

Peat is a soil composed almost entirely of very old vegetable matter. Usually it is sour — that is to say it is deficient in lime. However, when dressed with lime it can become extremely fertile. It is usually somewhat greyish in colour, unlike the dark peat dug out of marshy districts for fuel. Certain plants, such as some heathers, have adapted themselves to the acid conditions of peat, and will not grow in an ordinary fertile soil where lime is present.

Marl is a soil which contains carbonate of lime. Clayey marls are very fertile.

Humus is the name given to any decaying animal or vegetable matter in the soil.

Soil is generally referred to as either **heavy** or **light. Light** soil is loose and sandy. It is less arduous to dig than a heavy soil, and the spade will go into it fairly easily. Light soil is not usually so fertile as a heavy soil. **Heavy** soil is mainly clay, and retains more moisture than light soil. Heavy soil is certainly much harder to dig than the sandy light soil.

SOIL FERTILITY

All soil, heavy or light, needs to be brought into good condition by improving its natural texture. The treatment of both soils is somewhat similar, for both will benefit from the addition of humus. This can be accomplished by·working into the soil all the available dead leaves and plant tops, and digging in stable manure. On heavy soil the manure should be of a coarse nature, (containing straw) whereas the manure added to light soil should be heavier. The effect of adding humus in this way is to make heavy soil lighter and more porous, and light soils heavier and more able to retain moisture. Such materials can be incorporated into the soil during the process of bastard tranching.

Soil fertility depends not so much upon the amount of plant food in the soil as upon the food which is readily available to the roots. Plant food can only be taken up by the roots in a soluble form, and the insoluble plant food in the soil is, therefore, of little use.

The three main plant foods are **phosphates, nitrogen** and **potash.** They each have their own special function, and are essential for every kind of plant, other essential plant foods are present in sufficient quantities in most soils. They include sulphates, iron, magnesia, soda, chlorides, silica, oxygen and, of course, water.

Phosphates encourage the production of flowers.They are useful in the flower garden and orchard, where they can be freely applied.

Nitrogen is the leaf-forming food. It encourages quick development of the leaves and stems, and makes the plant grow larger. In the flower garden it should be used with care. If applied too liberally to flowers of any kind, the effect will be to produce a large, leafy plant, and possibly delay the flowers appearing.

Potash is a kind of tonic. It assists the plant to resist disease, and is essential to its health.

To be fully effective, these three plant foods require the presence of lime in the soil.

Lime is essential to most soils, the exceptions being soils in which lime-hating plants *(called Calcifuges)* are to be grown. The Rhododendron, and many heathers, are lime-haters. Lime is best applied in the form of slaked lime, during the late autumn or winter months. It should be spread evenly over the surface of the soil, where it can be left to be washed in by the rains. It is not advisable to use lime during the growing season, for it is liable to burn the plant foliage. For this reason, it is better to use a fine powder, which can be dusted over the surface of the soil without harming the plant leaves. Always apply lime to any vacant plot which has been deeply dug.

Having cleared the site of all unwanted material and vegetation, thoroughly and deeply dug the soil, and, finally, learnt something of the composition of soil and how to condition it, some consideration can be given to planning the envisaged garden layout.

5

Fig. 2.1 A Formal Garden (see 2-2 plan)

Chapter 2

DESIGNING THE GARDEN

MAKING A ROUGH SKETCH OF THE PLOT

Obviously, the first thing to do is to look at the plot. If it is an ordinary rectangular-shaped plot it will prove a simple matter to sketch a rough outline with boundary measurements. If, on the other hand, the plot is at all odd shaped, it will be as well to carefully prepare a drawing, to scale, setting down the irregular shape of the boundaries and their respective measurements.

Next, examine the lay of the land, and notice whether the surface is flat or sloping. The best views from the windows will be seen if the garden slopes down to the house, but if it slopes away from the house, the best views will be from the lower end of the slope looking towards the house. Any steepish or abrupt slope should therefore be noted, and a sectional drawing made showing the position and, if possible, the angle and depth of the fall or slopes.

Another point which will need to be noted, and marked upon the drawing, is the position of any trees or other features which are to be incorporated into the garden scheme. Also, if there is any unsightly building, either on or off the land, this should be indicated. If the final picture is not to be marred, steps will need to be taken to screen the offensive sight. Any attractive view should be noted, if it is likely to remain unspoilt, so that it can be left open to view, and thereby become part of the scene which is to be created.

Certain trees may cause future problems in the water garden, and should be noted. The leaves and/or berries of laburnum, laurel, holly and rhododendron will, if they enter the water and start to decompose, release poisons which will kill any fish. For this reason, such trees are best avoided if possible.

PREPARING A SCALE DRAWING

Having collected, as far as possible, all the information regarding the particular plot of land which is to be converted into a garden — including a note of the Northern compass point — the planning can be carried out indoors. Armed with pencil, eraser and a sheet of squared graph-paper, a start can be made designing the planned lay-out. Here, of course, your own ideas, personal taste and artistic ability will show themselves in the final scheme.

Fortunately no two gardens will be exactly alike, and it would be undesirable if they were. For one thing, no two people will have the same ideals regarding a garden; for another, it is seldom that two garden plots will be identical in all respects. In general the average, small, front garden, of a residence is seldom suitable for the creation of a water garden, although it may accommodate a small, ornamental pool and/or rockery. However, many back gardens can be converted into a water garden of one form or another. Such gardens may be either of formal or informal design, depending upon one's personal preference and the surroundings of the plot.

FORMAL AND INFORMAL GARDENS

The purist will insist that the style of the garden must be suited to the style of the house architecture. For instance, a modern, stream-lined house of severe design should have its gardens laid out on corresponding severe, streamlined, lines. On the other hand, cottage-style properties should have gardens of purely informal design. Whilst there is much to be said for this approach, the amateur gardener should follow his own instincts and preferences. Nevertheless, the completed garden should give pleasure to its creator, and be attractive to beholders; it should not require long hours of relentless attention, but be manageable with a few pleasurable hours each week, as necessary.

In this respect it must be said that the water garden will require far less attention than the terrestrial areas. The main tasks of maintenance being confined to the end of the season, it could be said that the water garden is the ideal for those who have little time to devote to the upkeep of the more usual type of garden. One can add to this the attraction which water has for most people, and the undoubted pleasure of relaxing beside a pool after a day's work. In the balm of a summer evening one can sit and contemplate the lazily gliding forms of the fish, as they swim below the pads of water-lilies with their gently bobbing, globular flowers. Around this tranquil scene the air is delicately perfumed with the scent of vanilla, arising from the flowers of the water hawthorn plants. Surely no ordinary garden can offer such delightful pleasures and demand so little attention in return.

Fig. 2.2 Plan of Formal Garden which incorporates informal borders and
tall Cupressus to enhance the depth

Fig. 2.3   Informal Pool with Moving Water

FEATURES TO INCLUDE

The informal water garden can incorporate a rill of rippling water, connecting one or more pools. Marsh and bog areas; rockeries of various types and sizes; areas of scree; shrub and heather gardens and so on, all set in a surround of grass with access paths of one sort or another.

The formal type of water garden is one of tamed-lines. It may be a single circular, ovoid, square or oblong-shaped pool, or it may be a series of such pools, each having a similarity to the others. The setting may be some form of paving or closely mowed grass, surrounded by well clipped low hedges. There may be rose beds, or some other herbaceous plantings, set in severe beds, in keeping with the overall design.

Despite the preference of the gardener, there is no doubt that the dimensions of the site will have some bearing upon, and may even dictate, the style of the garden. A walled courtyard, for instance, would be most unsuitable for an informal garden. It would, however, prove an ideal setting for a formal pool set in paving, surrounded by ornamental containers of various plants, and, possibly, a vine trained up the wall face, with the scene being illuminated at night, if desired, by a few judiciously placed coloured spotlights of the type specially manufactured for this purpose.

FURTHER DESIGN PRINCIPLES

Themes for the design of a garden are many and varied, just as the nature of man. It is up to the ingenuity of the individual to produce a garden design which is both pleasing and feasible, befitting the size and possibilities of the plot for which a lay-out is to be planned.

From the earlier sketches, transfer the outline of the plot to the graphpaper. The boundaries, and measurements, should be drawn as accurately as possible, and all other relevant features indicated in their correct positions. In the same way, re-draw any sectional sketches. Make the drawings to scale, and as large as possible. The larger the drawing, the easier it will be work upon. When satisfied that the detail of the plan is correctly set out, carefully ink over the pencil lines. Black ink will give permanence to the essential detail during the initial planning stages. If the final work-plan of the garden design has all existing features and boundaries drawn in black, and proposed new work in red, it will make the drawing much easier to understand, especially if a third party is involved during the construction work.

Pleasant hours can now be spent planning the garden, as the various features are lightly sketched in. It is seldom that the first drawing will prove entirely satisfactory, and a number of revisions are usually necessary before the ideal scheme is finally produced. Trial and error, draw and re-draw is the method most calculated to win the desired result for the average amateur. It is far easier to correct a design fault on paper than it is later, in the garden.

Whilst setting out the design certain principles must be borne in mind. In general, it is safe to say that a garden should present an attractive picture where no one feature dominates, but each blends to form a harmonious whole. If the site is large enough to allow more than a single garden theme, formal areas should be created nearest to the house. Informal areas should be placed further away from the house. Although occasionally the positions of these two types of garden can be reversed, there should be a natural progression from one to the other — possibly by passing through a rose garden. Water gardens have one common characteristic: water runs downhill. Therefore, if more than one pool is to be constructed, the largest pool should normally be situated at the bottom of a slope. Apart from these considerations, some allowance should be made for washing to be dried within easy proximity to the house.

Although not absolutely essential, the ideal would be to ensure that any brickwork blends with that of the house. This creation of harmony should be kept in mind when buying any new materials, or designing a new structure. Where space permits, a paved patio with pergola, decorated with ornamental containers of flowers, and pillar roses bedecking the pergola, will link the house to the garden, and provide a natural progression from one to the other.

ROCKS, PATHS AND STEPS

Rocks, in nature, occur as natural outcrops mostly, so rockeries should, when possible, follow this same principle. If the land is flat and has no fall, it may be worthwhile moving soil from one area to another to form slight slopes and shallow terraces. The material obtained when excavating for pools, rills or other sunken features can also be utilised in the creation of varying ground levels. Whenever soil is moved in this manner, the fertile 10 inches (254mm) of top-soil should first be removed. Form the contours from the subsoil, and then replace the top-soil over the altered area of ground.

Fig. 2.4 **Top** Pool and Loggia
Bottom Before Improvements Effected

13

Rocks can be built up to form a background to a pool, or edge an area of bank by a stream or rill. They might be employed to form a rockery between two terrace levels — if the difference in height between each is sufficient — thus retaining the higher level. Low terraces can be separated and retained by constructing dry-stone walling.

The provision of paths must not be overlooked. They can take many forms and be constructed from various materials, but all have the common aim of providing a firm, safe, drained footway from one place to another, even if they are nothing more than comfortably spaced slabs set in grass. Normally a path should be of sufficient width to enable two people to walk side by side. It should be firmly based, and well drained, providing safe, dry footage during inclement weather. It must be well-made, and strong enough to withstand usage over many years, unless it is to need regular attention. It should also be capable of supporting a laden wheel-barrow when necessary.

Where the ground slopes, or has terraces, some form of steps will be required. However the steps are made, they need to be constructed with at least as much care as a path. In order to safely accommodate the foot, each tread should be no less that 13 to sixteen inches (330-406mm) deep, overhanging the one below it by about two inches (50.80mm). The rise, or height between each step, should be no more than six inches (152.40mm). Long, continuous flights of steps should be avoided; where more than ten steps are to be built it is advisable to incorporate a resting place in the form of a landing. In some situations such a landing might be a suitable place for a seat to be placed, upon which the less agile might rest.

Greenhouses and frames, sheds, compost heaps and rubbish-dumps are very often a visual distraction. Anything which is likely to be an ugly eyesore is better hidden from sight, surrounded by some form of screen. An excellent way of screening is to erect trellis, up which is trained suitable roses or climbing clematis. Ugly brickwork can be hidden in a similar manner by tacking trellis to the wall. It is not necessary for the trellis to form a close screen — it can have foot square openings between the laths.

Although many of the materials used in the construction of rock and water gardens are dealt with in other chapters, there are some other general points which should not be overlooked, even while the first sketch of the garden is being made.

Certain areas of the garden may require, by their nature, more attention than others. For instance, unless grass is given constant attention in order to preserve its appearance, it will quickly assume an uncared for look. It will need regular cutting and rolling, and,

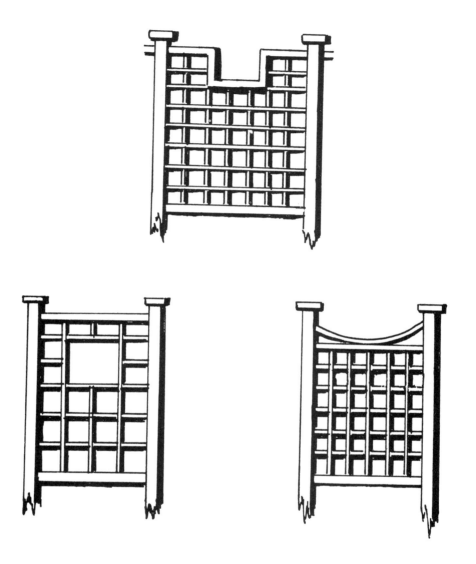

Fig. 2.5   Screen Panels
Three types of trellis design

15

although modern equipment allows this to be done with a minimum of labour, it is most important that the task is not neglected at any time. Therefore, unless the necessary time and attention can be given, grassed areas should be kept to a minimum. An excellent, and fragrant, substitute is chamomile. Chamomile plants are evergreen, and create lawns which do not need cutting. When walked upon, plants crushed underfoot will release a pleasant fragrance. Other alternatives to a lawn are paved areas, banks of shrubs and heather or ground covering planted areas.

The most effective gardens are those where simplicity is the over-riding element in its design, and fussiness is carefully avoided. Nothing can be truly beautiful which appears to be inappropriate, or which is badly-managed and uncared for. These points mean that the design conception should be simple and straightforward, including nothing unless it really does benefit the garden scheme. If labour is short, it should be planned with this fact in mind, so the design ensures that the garden will require only a minimum of attention to preserve its attractions.

The drawings which accompany this chapter are intended as no more than ideas, and serve merely to suggest how to plan a water garden of either formal or informal design. When setting out the desired scheme, it will be found that the best approach is to commence by sketching-in the pool, or pools, and any waterways first. Next, add such features as marsh or bog areas, followed by rockeries. If it has been decided to terrace the plot, it will now be possible to draw the necessary contour lines (in the form of dotted lines), the logical positions being indicated by the positions of various features, which will also suggest possible waterfall sites.

Having arranged the "backbone" of the garden, such essentials as paths, retaining walls, screens and paved areas can be added. Finally, complete the plan by indicating lawns, rose beds and any other proposed decorative of floral areas. To avoid any later confusion, ensure that all features are clearly indentified as the plan develops.

Where possible, a similar approach can be made to the actual construction of the garden. By first digging out the pools and any other sunken areas, it becomes much easier to dipose of the excavated material over the surrounding ground. The disposal of such material (which can be very considerable) in an existing garden can present quite a problem.

Before bringing this chapter to a close, it is worth suggesting that, if finances are sufficient and the site is accessible, the hire of a contractor with suitable machinery should be given serious consideration.

Fig. 2.6 Steps can be Incorporated Into the Design

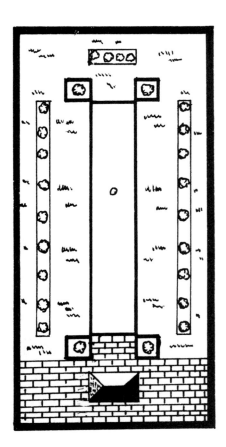 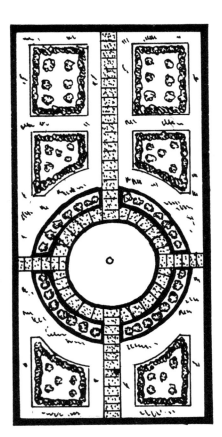

Fig. 2.7   Formal Garden Styles

Left: Paved area with summer house overlooking canal, with centre fountain and four ornamental flower containers, set in grass and flanked by rose borders
Right: Italian style. A circular pool, with fountain, raised above ground level and separated from the surrounding raised flower bed with paved paths. The small beds contain roses and have clipped dwarf hedges

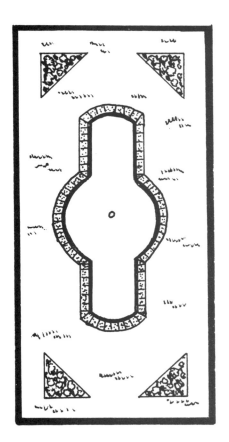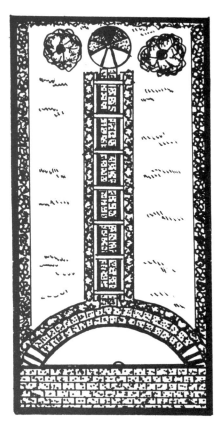

Fig. 2.8   Formal Garden Styles (cont.)

Left: A simple design with triangular flower beds. The pool has a centre fountain and is surrounded by a paved path
Right: A raised, paved terrace leads down to the pool into which a wall-fountain splashes. From the pool a path leads, beneath a pergola, to a circular sun arbour which is flanked by two ornamental trees. The borders are filled with flowers, whilst climbing roses clamber over the pergola

19

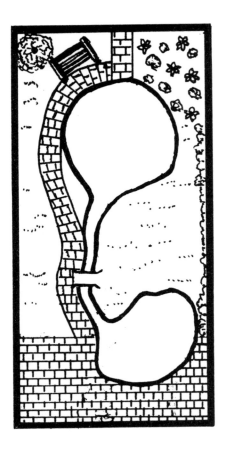 

Fig. 2.9 Informal Gardens

Left: A paved area and path leads to a seat, behind which is an ornamental tree. The upper pool runs along a stream, beneath a bridge, into the lower pool. The top right-hand corner contains shrubs. Along the right-hand boundary there is a hedge of lavender
Right: Stepping stones are set into the lawn, passing ornamental trees on the left, to steps which lead to the high level. The upper pool tumbles over the rockery in a waterfall, to the lower pool. Along the right-hand side is a bed of various shrubs, which is raised above lawn level and fronted by a dry-stone wall

 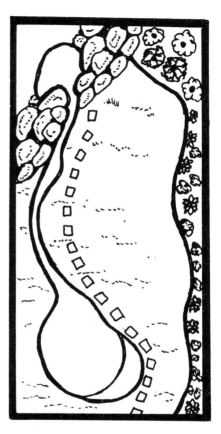

Fig. 2.10 Informal Gardens (cont.)

Left: From the moraine, in the top right-hand corner, a waterfall cascades down the rockery into a pool, runs into a stream which is flanked on the left by a marshy area. The stream passes a bridge to enter a lower pool, which is surrounded by crazy paving. Near the ornamental tree stepping stones lead to a small crazy paved area adjoining the rockery. Ornamental shrubs occupy the right-hand boundary position
Right: A long dry-wall bed, on the right, contains shrubs and ornamental trees. From a small upper pool a waterfall tumbles over the rockery into a stream which runs into the lower pool

21

The early prepratory work, creating differing levels and digging out large pools, is extremely hard work and should not be undertaken lightly by any but the perfectly fit. The hire of a skilled contractor will save many hours of very hard labour, and avoid the possibility of physical aches and pains. The larger the area of land, the more a contractor becomes worthy of his hire, the cost being amply repaid in the later pleasure of enjoying the landscaped garden.

Chapter 3

POOLS AND WATER FEATURES

REFLECTIONS

There can be few things so pleasing to the human senses as the gentle splash of water falling from a fountain, the gurgle of a splashing waterfall, or to watch the rainbow reflections of sunshine as the water drops onto the surface of a pool. It is pleasant to sit, after a hot summer day, and quietly contemplate the cool, placid water, and the grace of the colourful fish as they glide below the surface. The cares of the day can be slowly forgotten, at least for a time, as one marvels at the waxen beauty of the lightly nodding flowers of the water lily. Caressed by the zephyr-like touch of an evening breeze, the water hawthorn yields its delicate perfume to the air, and the reed-like plants rustle and chatter in subdued manner amongst themselves. Surely there can be few who would not be enchanted by the magical charm of the well-made ornamental pool, when at its best.

Even when it is not accompanied by any type of aquatic planting, water can give an added interest to a garden. During the hot days of summer, merely to sit beside a rippling rill of clear shallow water, is an attraction hard to resist.

Water becomes a focal point, therefore it must attract and charm the eye of the beholder. To succeed, the planning and execution requires careful attention at all stages — it is not enough to simply dig a hole and/or channels, line with some waterproof material, and fill with water. If it is to be successful, the right position must be chosen, the size and shape carefully thought out, the method of construction decided, and proper attention given to its execution.

SITUATION

Water should always be in an open position, away from trees, where it can enjoy the benefit of sunshine. The full charm of water will not be seen if it never reflects the sunlight. Overhanging trees will cause problems. The roots will reach for the cool moisture of a concrete type pool; the willow and poplar are notorious for their abil-

Fig. 3.1 Formal Settings
Top: Ground level pool set in lawn and flanked by shrub beds
Bottom: Raised pool in an enclosed area

ity to damage even the foundations of a house, and they may eventually cause the pool structure to fracture. Leaves can also be a problem — they will fall into the water and decompose, and, if allowed to accumulate excessively, will greatly pollute the water, to the danger of any fish. Some trees, such as laburnum, laurel, holly and rhododendrons, have poisonous leaves and berries which are toxic to fish; in particular the seeds which follow the flowers of the laburnum are very dangerous — they contain the water-soluble poison cytisine. This alkaloid can make a child very ill if the seeds are put into the mouth.

On the whole, therefore, it is better to site water in a fairly open position, away from trees, although a wall or raised rockery can be used as a "back-cloth" to afford some shade from the heat of a hot mid-day sun, or to protect the pool from the harsh northerly and easterly winds. Unless sunlight reaches the pool for at least part of the day, the water-plants will not prosper, and the pool will degenerate into dark, stagnant water. Whereas it is always possible to shade a pool which receives too much light, it would be much more difficult to bring light to one in permanent shade.

A water garden can be either formal or informal in design.

FORMAL WATER GARDENS

In the formal design, pools may be sunk flush with the surrounding land, or raised by being built on the land surface; or they may be part below and part above ground level. They must be geometrically shaped, and are usually rectangular, square or circular. Any canals or rills normally follow straight lines.

A formal canal may form the sole water feature, or be used as a connecting link between pools. It is at its most pleasing when the length is emphasized rather than its width. There are numerous examples of canals built on the grand scale, that of the Taj Mahal being but one of many.

Geometrically-shaped pools and straight lined canals require a centrepiece — figure, plant or fountain spray — which stands well above the pool structure. The surrounding area should be one of paving, close clipped lawn or precision cut hedges; regimented rose beds or herbacious borders; ornamental plant containers, or brick walls, the whole blending into strictly controlled lines, where formality alone reigns supreme. Informality has no place in such a scene.

25

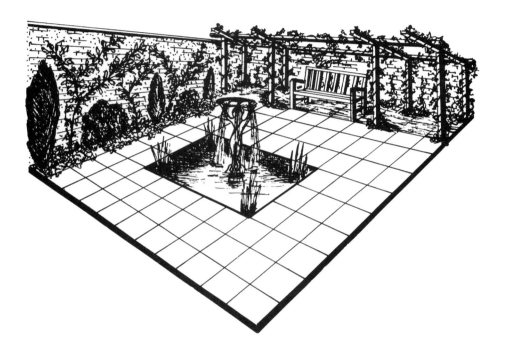

Fig. 3.2 Simple Formality

Small, walled gardens can be made attractive if the design is planned carefully. Paving provides an area for outdoor meals, whilst the pergola gives shade for a garden seat. The brickwork is softened by the use of climbing and other plants and the pool adds interest to the scene

FOUNTAINS

Apart from fountains in the water, it is possible to employ a so-called "wall fountain" in the design of the formal water garden. Basically, this is nothing more than a jet of water projected from a wall, through some form of ornamentation — often the face of a lion or gargoyle, the water emerging from the mouth in the form of either a trickle or a jet, to fall into the pool.

Fountains, whether of the wall or common pool type, are really only suitably for the formal pool. They may be used with equal success in both the large garden and that of more limited dimensions. They are, in fact, the ideal way of introducing water movement in the formal pool in a visually attractive manner. Care must be taken to ensure that the size of the fountain jet does not exceed the length or width of the pool. A fountain spray that constantly splashes over on to the pathway is an unwelcome nuisance. For the same reason it is not wise to place a fountain where there is much wind, which may carry spray to the surrounding paths. Regulate the height of the jet, or otherwise control the radius of the falling fountain spray, to avoid this problem.

Probably the commonest type of fountain is the central, single jet design. This may rise from the water surface or from some type of ornamental figure or sculptured design raised above the water surface. However, it is possible to vary the theme by employing a multi-jet fountain-head to create a variety of falling spray patterns. In general, the fountain head is positioned in the pool in such a way that it is just above the surface of the water, the multi-jet usually being placed in the centre of the pool.

ELECTRIC PUMPS

Although it is possible to operate a fountain by the use of mains water, it is more usual nowadays to install an electrically operated pump. The most popular type of pump is fully submersible and can be purchased complete with a fountain-head, or as a combined fountain and waterfall kit. The height of the fountain-throw is dependent upon the power of the pump — the average pump has sufficient capacity to throw a fountain jet to a height of around 6 feet (1.83m), and can usually be adjusted by a built-in flow regulator. At this height the approximate spread of the fall would be a radius of around 4 feet (1.22m), and this should be taken into account when positioning the fountain in the pool.

Fig. 3.3 An Informal Garden
The informal water garden should appear to be a creation of Nature

If mains water is to operate the fountain, it will be necessary to arrange an overflow outlet to enable the surplus water to be carried away and, preferably, discharged into the main drainage system. It will also require the installation of pipework during the construction of the garden and pool, for both water supply and drainage, in order to hide them from sight. In this connection it must be stressed most strongly that copper pipe must not be used. Copper, especially new copper, is extremely poisonous to fish and has caused many losses. Where possible, make all waterpipe installations in plastic to avoid any possible risk to the well-being of any fish — this applies to both inlet and outlet piping.

INFORMAL WATER GARDENS

Possibly the most informal type of garden is the apparently wild garden, where the whole garden is cunningly devised to give the impression of land where the hand of Nature rules supreme. Wild and semi-wild plants grow in profusion, attracting butterflies to the area during the sunny days, the air being enlivened by the sound of bees busily going about their business of gathering nectar. Man-made features, as with the control which must be exercised, are not allowed to become blatantly obvious — man's work must blend into the scene, so that the illusion is preserved. Such gardens are not usually suitable for the small plots of the modern home.

The more usual type of informal garden relies upon a minimum, or a complete absence, of straight lines. The outlines of pools, streams, borders and so on follow unregimented curves, whilst the land may be formed into varying levels of undulation, although it can be flat, especially if it has a slight fall. It is, however, essential that all irregularities in outline should be carefully planned to add beauty — they must not appear to be erratic.

To give a natural aspect, the pools should be sunk level with the surrounding ground and any streams or rills should vary in width. Needless to say, marsh and bog gardens should be situated near to one or other of the water features. Rock-gardens can be constructed along the banks of waterways, as backgrounds to pools, or to retain one land-level above lower ground, and in similar positions to appear as natural outcrops of rock. With some modification, follow nature's design methods.

It is possible, if the plot is very small, to create a cross between the formal and informal, although purists would not approve. The pool can be arranged in a kidney-like shape, with a low, raised surrounding

Fig. 3.4   The Informal Water Garden

wall. Behind can be a rockery down which a waterfall tumbles into the pool. Set in paving or close-cropped lawn, this arrangement can make a most attractive feature within a fairly limited area of garden.

WATER CIRCULATION

The movement of water is accomplished either by the injection of mains water, or by using a pump to circulate the water from a lower pool to one set at a higher level. The latter is the more usual method, the rate at which the water flows depending upon the power of the pump. Whichever method is used it will, for the sake of neatness and appearance, require that the water circulation pipes be hidden from sight. A point to remember is that the end of all circulation pipes, at the higher level, must be kept above the pool water level. Should this point not be observed, and the inlet be placed below water, there is a great risk that in the event of the circulation system failing, or being temporarily discontinued, a syphon effect will be created which will empty the water from the higher pool down to the level of the open pipe. For this reason no pipe which conducts water to a lower level should be submerged at its highest end. However, the lower end of such a pipe can be placed below water, because, whereas water will run downhill, it will not run uphill without some form of assistance.

The lowest pool should be fitted with an adequate overflow, to carry water away to a suitable drainage point. This is essential if mains water is used to circulate the water, and very necessary during heavy, prolonged rain storms, to avoid the pool overflowing and flooding the surrounding area.

Waterfalls should not be arranged into a series of identical steps, resembling a stairway — instead they should vary in the height of fall and, if falling from one to another, slightly twist and turn through their flight. Disguise the hand of man as much as possible and let the water tumble as though nature had arranged its course.

OTHER FEATURES

Rockeries should be positioned where the various plants can enjoy the sunshine which they require; alpine type plants will seldom flourish if they are planted in a position which is in permanent shade. The rockery should be boldly planned, although it should not be allowed to unduly dominate the other features, and be constructed of large pieces of rock. Within reason, the larger the individual stones, the more impressive will the rockery appear. However, they should not be so large that they cannot be man-handled into the desired position safely.

Although wet, marshy areas should be adjacent to pools or streams, they should not be over-large. As with other areas of the garden, it will be necessary to attend to such matters as weeding, thinning or replacing plants, and so forth. For ease of maintenance it is always advisable to ensure that all parts of the bog or marsh garden are within easy reach, either from the surrounding firm ground, for from judiciously placed stepping stones.

Without appearing too contrived, paths or stepping stones should always provide firm, dry, safe footing when working on the various features of the water garden, apart from serving their purpose of leading to and from one part of the garden to another. Although not essential, a well-constructed path will often allow passage over an area of ground which has become sodden and waterlogged, however, briefly, due to natural or other causes. Such walk-ways are especially beneficial during the wetter months of the year, and will prevent the ruining of footwear to a large degree. Nevertheless, the planning of paths should be given careful consideration, for they must not detract from but, rather, blend into the surroundings as far as possible. In some instances it may be better to make use of stepping stones, instead of relying upon the more usual type of continuous path. Again, the choice of materal used in the construction may well help to make the path less conspicuous in its particular setting. For instance, by making use of suitable pieces of flat surfaced stone, similar to that used to make the rockery, it is possible to give the impression that the random stepping stones near the water are an extension of that rockery, being the exposed surfaces of a seam of buried rock.

The informal water garden, in a plot of average size, may consist of little more than a raised rockery down which a waterfall cascades to splash into an irregular shaped pool. From the pool a shallow stream burbles, tumbling over a bed of stones and rippling over low falls as the water finds its way between rock-edged, grassy banks, finally to leap over another waterfall into a lower pool. Along its course the stream swells into marshy areas — here tall plants nod and bow to the caress of the winds; in the stream bright splashes of colour from the golden, buttercup yellow flowers of Marsh Marigold and the blue of Water Forget-me-not; the water surface of the pools adorned by the bobbing, globular blossoms of the majestic water lily, whilst around the margins proudly stand the stiff sword-like leaves of the Water Iris as they unashamedly display their flowers for all to see. Set in close-cropped turf, or chamomile lawn, traversed by a gently curving path of stepping stones, this simple water garden scheme can be most attractive — if designed with care.

In the following chapters the various features, and their construction, will be considered in some detail. Equipment, plants and fish will also be covered. Because the creation of a garden is so much a work of personal choice and creation, it is up to the reader to decide which feature to incorporate into the final design. The pages which follow will merely, it is hoped, assist in that decision and try to guide the novice around likely pitfalls.

A SMALL ROCK GARDEN. THE LAYERS OF STONE ARE PLACED TO GIVE THE MOST NATURAL EFFECT POSSIBLE

33

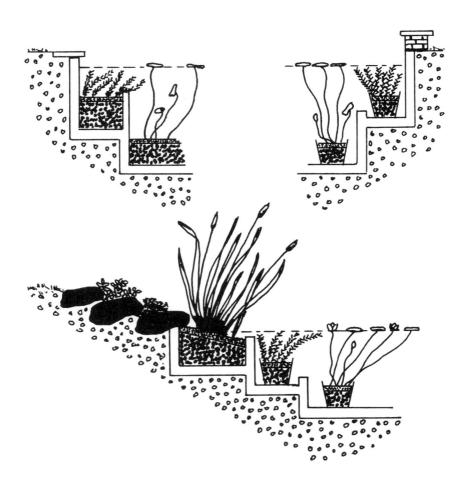

Fig. 4.1   Sections Through Pools
Top left: Paved surround, loam laid in troughs and over base
Top right: Dwarf wall surround. Plants set in containers
Botton: Rockery, marsh area, and plants in containers

Chapter 4

CONSTRUCTING THE WATERY SCENE

Whether the garden is of formal or informal design, the same care must be devoted to the construction of the water features. A badly constructed, poorly designed pool which suffers from water leakage will present the same problems in both cases. Careful attention through all stages will be amply repaid by an attractive, long-lasting, watertight feature, be it pool or stream.

SIZE OF POOLS

The dimensions of pools must also be carefully considered, and should, within reason, be as large as possible. A large pool will require less attention than one of smaller dimensions, and suffer less from water temperature fluctuations. Extreme variations in the temperature, if it fluctuates rapidly, may harm any fish and could result in their death. Such fish as Koi, which are large growing, reaching a body length of 2 feet (610mm) or more, will require much larger pools than such types as the smaller goldfish. The minimum depth of water for goldfish should not be less than 2 feet (610mm), whilst Koi should be allowed twice that depth. These water depths should be adequate to protect the fish during the average British winter, but could be increased if it is desired. Whatever depth is decided upon, the width and length should always be greater than the water depth.

CALCULATING THE NUMBER OF FISH

Fish breathe in oxygen which is dissolved in the water; oxygen is absorbed from the atmosphere, through the water surface, which also allows various noxious gas to escape. The larger the surface area of the water, the greater will be the number of fish that can safely be placed in the pool. It must always be the surface area which decides the number of fish and not, as many people wrongly believe, the amount of water. **There is a long established, well tried rule which allows a maximum of one inch (25mm) of fish, exluding the fins, to each 24 square inches (155cm^2) of water surface.** It must be stressed that this is maximum and, if young fish are being introduced, a reduc-

$6''/ft^2$

tion of up to fifty per cent would avoid any possibility of later over-crowding due to the growth of the fish.

PROVISION FOR PLANTS

Provision must be made for the plants by arranging suitable shelves in the pool. If it is intended to put the plants in containers — an increasingly popular method which simplifies pool maintenance — the shelves must be so positioned that the depth of the containers, plus the growing length of the submerged plants, is allowed for. If the plants are to be grown in a permanent position in the pool the shelves must contain lips raised sufficiently to be capable of holding a 3-4 inch (76-103mm) depth of compost in position. The thickest area of submerged plants, and thus the greatest area of shelving, should be at the shallow end of the pool — the ideal pool will have both a deep and shallow area. The fish prefer to spawn in shallow water, and, as the water is usually warmer, young fish will congregate in the heavily planted shallows and be protected by the vegetation. Unfortunately, most fish are cannibalistic and will eat their own eggs and any very small fish which can be caught. Even with the protection of plants many little fish will be lost; without them it is doubtful whether any would survive.

MARKING OUT THE POOL OUTLINE

If the advice given in the previous chapters has been followed, the rough preparatory work will have been attended to and a design plan for the garden prepared. From the drawing, mark out the position, shape and size of the pools, together with any waterways. The easy method is to pour dry sand to the life-size outline of these various features. If it is then felt that there should be some slight alteration, it is a simple matter to brush away the sand and re-mark the outline. Once satisfied, dig out a shallow trench around the sand-marked outline — this will act as a guide for the excavation work and prevent the outline being erased or lost.

EXCAVATION

If the work is to be constructed in concrete the excavation should follow the outline, but enlarged sufficiently to allow for the thickness of the material (otherwise the internal dimensions will be reduced accordingly); however, if a plastic liner is to be used no such allowance need be made.

The ideal time to undertake the construction of waterways and pools is during a spell of cool, dry, settled weather. Rain will create a muddy quagmire, and there is no pleasure in working under such conditions. Nor will a hot sun or cold wind be pleasant to work in. Concrete pools are best started during early autumn, before the frosts arrive; they can be completed before the onset of winter. With the arrival of spring the pool will be ready for a final clean and the waterways can be flushed through, the plants being placed in position early engough to allow them to become firmly rooted before any fish are introduced.

If the area of excavation is very large it could save a lot of aches and pains, to say the least, if a contractor and his machinery were engaged to carry out the work. Although expensive, the hire of a skilled contractor is certainly worthy of serious consideration — if the pocket will allow the expense.

Whether the work is delegated or undertaken as a self-imposed sentence of hard labour it will be necessary to decide where the excavated soil is to be put. The amount of soil will be considerable and it should be deposited well clear of the scene of operations, keeping the fertile top soil to one side. At a later stage the surplus soil might form the bais of a rockery.

As the work proceeds, work the excavations into the desired shapes, with shallow and deep areas together with plant shelves, but allowing if necessary for the thickness of the construction material. Streams should vary in width and depth; in nature wide areas are usually shallow, whilst narrow parts are deeper.

MATERIALS AND METHODS OF CONSTRUCTION

Concrete. If the pool is properly constructed this material will give one of the most permanent of artificial pools; it can be built to practically any size, shape or depth. Working with concrete requires a great deal of hard labour, but, in the years to come — long after the aches and pains have been forgotten — it will all have been worthwhile.

The simplest and easiest shape to construct is one which is saucer shaped with flattish, gently sloping walls. However, if the walls are nearly vertical, shuttering will be required to hold the concrete in position, and this should be very strongly constructed and braced to prevent it collapsing with the weight of the concrete. Spacers will be required to hold the shuttering at least 6 inches (152 mm) away from the inner face of the excavation. These spacers are removed after the concrete has been poured, and the concrete must be well tamped down to make sure that all air pockets are eliminated. The base is laid after the shuttering has been removed, but before the concrete has hardened too much, after which it is finished as described later.

Sloping walls will allows the concrete to be 'battered' into place, without the use of shuttering. This requires a stiff concrete mix, which is thrown firmly against the walls and base. It shoud be firm enough to stay in place, and is then battered with the back of a spade. Continue over the whole of the excavation, building a depth of around 3 inches (76 mm). The following day, repeat the process to build up the concrete to a thickness of 6 inches (152 mm). Any reinforcing material can be sandwiched between these two layers.

Whichever method is used the concrete mix should be in the proportion of **1 part cement, 2 parts clean sharp sand and three parts washed coarse ballast** — all measured with a bucket. Mix thoroughly in the dry state until the colour is uniform and free from streaks of grey or red. Make a depression in the agglomeration and then pour a little water on it. Continue mixing and adding a little more water as required. The concrete should not be too sloppy — a stiff consistency is required (and rather firmish if it is to be 'battered'). Test it by plunging and withdrawing the shovel — if it leaves ridges it is about right. The concrete must be laid as soon as possible after mixing.

Just as soon as the concrete has become firm, but not hard, a coat of the same concrete mix should be trowelled over to a thickness of 1 inch (25 mm); this layer need not be too smooth and is better left a little rough. The following day a finishing coat should be applied to a thickness of ½-1 inch (13-25 mm).

This finishing coat, which is rendered over the complete face of the concrete and trowelled to a smooth finish, is a stiff mix composed of **1 part cement to 3 parts clean sharp sand,** plus a **waterproofing powder,** added according to the manufacturer's instructions. This rendering must be completed in one operation, care being taken to eliminate any air bubbles that may appear. When this final coat has set firm, cover it with damp sacks or something similar, to slow down the drying period. Within reason, the longer concrete takes to dry the harder it will be. Allow the concrete to harden for a week before introducing any water.

It is possible to estimate the amount of concrete required for the foregoing mixes by allowing approximately **13 cubic feet (0.36 m^3) of cement, 26 cu. ft. (0.74 m^3) of sand, and 38.6 cu. ft. (1.1 m^3) of ballast**

for each 100 square feet (9.3 m^2) of 6 inch (152 mm) thick concrete.
Calculating the pool area is done by measuring the length and width
and adding twice the maximum depth to each. The two figures are
then multiplied together to arrive at the square footage. To convert
cubic feet into cubic yards, divide by 27.

CEMENT BLOCK AND BRICK CONSTRUCTION

These are ideal for the construction of raised, formal type pools.
If the pool is to be partly below, and partly above, ground level, the
base should first be laid to a depth of 6 inches (152 mm), taking care
that no soil falls into the excavation. The walls are then built on this
foundation, to the required height above the ground. Where the pool
is to be entirely above ground, first make a form from battens slightly
larger than the outside measurements of the pool. Pour a 1:2:3 concrete mix into the form to act as a 6 inch (152 mm) thick foundation
and base, making sure that it is level in all directions.

Whether concrete blocks or hard house bricks are used, they
should be thoroughly soaked in water before use. Lay a line of mortar
onto the conrete base after it has set, and commence laying the walls.
For obvious reasons, use a spirit level during this work until the
required height is reached, and leave the inside joints a little rough
to act as a key for the rendering. The outside can, however, be neatly
pointed, unless the exterior is also to be rendered over.

Allow the mortar to set for a day before applying the rendering to
the base and walls in one complete operation, as described for concrete pools. At this stage any capping can also be placed into position.
It may be that, prior to rendering, the interior surfaces will require
wetting — rendering is not very successful if laid on a dry surface,
and is liable to break away with time. Cover the completed work, to
delay the hardening process, and leave for a week.

ELIMINATING LIME

New concrete contains a considerable quantity of lime, which must
be eliminated before it is safe. Lime is highly toxic and will prove
fatal to most fish and water plants. It is possible to apply various sea-
lants to the concrete faces, to prevent lime entering the water. However, if these coatings become damaged the lime will be waiting to
leak into the water with predictable results.

The oldest, and safest method requires a little more hard work,
but after the effort put into building the pool, surely a litte more

Fig. 4.2 Construction Methods

Top: Plastic liner laid over layer of sand and tucked under paving surround

Bottom: Shuttering and bracing to retain concrete, until it sets ready for rendering

energy can be found to complete the job! Fill the pool with water and leave for a week , then, with a stiff brush, throughly scrub it all over. The pool is then emptied and any sediment removed. Refill and leave for a few days before repeating the process of scrubbing and emptying. When there is no longer any trace of the white-coloured sediment, it will be reasonable to assume that the concrete has been rendered safe. The safety of the pool can be checked for certain by placing an inexpensive fish into the pool. If at the end of a week, it survives, it will prove beyond doubt that the pool is safe. However, if the fish dies it will indicate that the concrete needs more curing, to remove the final traces of lime.

CONSTRUCTION WITH PLASTICS

The modern method of constructing pools entails the use of plastic sheeting; this method is much less arduous than mixing and pouring concrete, and allows the pools to be put into immediate use. Some plastics are longer lived than others, and it is this factor which decides the suitability of the particular sheeting and the ultimate life expectancy of the pool. Great care must be taken to avoid puncturing the material, for even the smallest pin-prick will cause a water leakage that will be difficult to trace. Broadly speaking, there are three types of plastic material that can be used as pool-liners.

Polythene is the cheapest and least safisfactory. It has the great disadvantage of deteriorating after a few years; it rots above the water-line where it is exposed to the effects of air and sunlight. This material is only suitable for temporary use and should be at least 500 gauge quality, and preferably black, which has a slightly longer life than the clear type.

P.V.C. is much more suitable as a liner — it is tougher than polythene and is often reinforced with a nylon mesh. This material wears well and has a greater resistance to being punctured; it is often available with a pebble dash design on one side and plain blue on the other.

Butyl is the most expensive type of liner and also the most suitable. It is tough, with an almost indefinite life, and is, or should be, virtually trouble free. Butyl has a great advantage in that it is possible to join it by electric welding, or the use of a special adhesive and tape, to create various sizes and shapes. It is a black rubber-like material.

Being flexible, plastic liners, unlike concrete, are not affected by ground movement, freezing, or the effects of contraction and expansion caused by temperature fluctuations.

In order to determine the size of liner required, the length and width of the excavation should be measured. Measure the maximum width of the base plus the height of the opposing walls. Taken from the deepest section of the excavation, then repeat for the length. To these measurements add an additional 2 feet (610 mm) — this will allow an all-round overlap of 12 inches (305 mm), which will be hidden beneath the pool surrounds.

Having prepared the excavation, carefully remove any stones or other sharp material that might make a hole in the liner. Next line the excavation with a thick, protective layer of soft sand, old carpet pieces, layers of newspapers or similar material, as a precaution against punctures. Stretch the liner over the site of the pond, then allow it to drape down into the excavation, checking that there is an equal overlap all round.

The pond can now be slowly filled with water through a garden hose. As the weight of the water pulls the liner down, and moulds it to the shape of the pool, gently pull and ease the liner into position, trying to disguise any folds or creases that may form. Care at this stage will add much to the appearance of the finished pool. Place weights around the overlap, to prevent it falling into the water, until it can be held permanently in position by the surround.

If the liner is being used in a raised pool, the interior surfaces should be given a very smooth finish and the overlap held in position by the wall capping. The informal pool can have the overlap buried beneath turves or a surrounding path.

Canals, streams and rills are all treated in the same manner as the pool. Be sure that, in the case of canals and pools, levels are maintained — nothing looks worse than a formal pool in which the water appears to slope, due to the walls not being level. Varying levels in the banks of informal pools and streams can be disguised by the use of rockwork, which will add to the informal aspect. It will, of course, be necessary to lower a section of the surrounding bank if the pool is to overflow into a stream or waterfall.

FIBREGLASS POOLS

These are available in various preformed shapes and sizes. They tend to be rather expensive and seldom have sufficient depth, even in the event that there might be a reasonable area of water surface. In fact, most are hardly large enough for the well-being of fish. Installation merely requires a hole of sufficient size to accommodate the moulding, placing it in position, and, after levelling, firming the soil around it.

PLUMBING

In-flow and out-flow plumbing, if any, should be built in during the construction work. Modern plastic plumbing pipes and fittings make this a fairly simple operation, if it is given a little thought. Incorporating an overflow will prevent problems if the pool is filled beyond its capacity and will also prevent the water rising above a certain level. Set the overflow at least 6 inches (152 mm) below the top level of the pool, and the water should not rise beyond that point. The overflow need be nothing more than a hole which penetrates the pool wall, or a pipe which connects to another leading to a main drainage point. A standpipe, however, would be more useful. A socket is built into the base of the pool and a standpipe, of the required length to suit the desired water level, is pushed into the socket. The pipe will prevent the water rising above it and, if removed, will allow the pool to be drained. The socket should be very firmly fitted into the pool base and lead to a main drainage point or something similar. Needless to say, all connections must be perfectly watertight — again the local plumbers merchant should be able to supply suitable connector sockets and pipes, but they must be plastic and not metal. **Some metals, such as copper and brass, can release poisons into the water, especially when new, which will kill any fish.**

BOG AND MARSH GARDENS

These are best seen in conjunction with the informal pool or alongside a stream, where the natural contour can be followed, as such wet areas do in nature, in close proximity to the water. This is the ideal setting for many of the beautiful pond-side plants that enjoy marshy conditions, such as the irises, reeds and rushes.

The easiest method of constructing an area of bog is to allow for it when building the pool or stream. Build the section of pool or stream oversize, extending it to incorporate the area which will become the marsh area, in the form of a shallow depression. This shallow portion needs to be of sufficient depth to allow a 6 inch (152 mm) layer of clinker or broken bricks and stones, plus a topping of 6 inches (152 mm) of loam and a final 2 inch (51 mm) dressing of clean gravel or chippings. It follows, therefore, that the minimum depth of the bog must be 14 inches (356 mm). If the pond is constructed in concrete, the excavation depth will need to be 22 inches (550 mm), to allow for the thickness of the concrete. When the concrete rendering has been completed, build an irregular barrier (in keeping with the pond outline), leaving holes for the water to penetrate into the bog area.

Ponds lined with plastic sheeting require slightly different treatment, but are equally uncomplicated. Leave a barrier of soil between the pool and the bog-garden — this should be dished slightly along its upper edge so that it allows water from the pool to overflow. The liner is purchased large enough to line both the pool and bog garden in one sheet. Alternatively, it can be treated in the same way as for a concrete construction, by building a barrier of rockwork. In this case it is adviseable to bed the base of the rocks in concrete — which will need to be cured — so that they are held firmly in position.

It is essential that some form of barrier is created in order to retain the planting medium and prevent it washing into the water.

FILTERS

If it is thought necessary a filter system can be incorporated to help maintain water clarity. Many of those enthusiasts who specialize in keeping Koi insist that an efficient filtration system is essential, due to the large size of these fish and their habit of stirring up the bottom sediment. Two methods are commonly used, one internal, the other external.

The internal filter will require that the depth of the pool is increased by 12-18 inches (305-457 mm). A frame, equal in size to at least one third of the water surface area, is constructed from rigid ¾ inch (19 mm) bore plastic pipe, 'T' pieces and elbows. The straight lengths should be drilled with ¼ inch (6 mm) holes; the distance between the holes should gradually decrease the further they are from the pump connection point. Space the long pipes about 8 inches (203 mm) apart, joining them at each end by shorter drilled pieces, to span the pool base. Make a connecting point for the pump by inserting into the frame a 'T' piece to which a length of hosepipe has been joined. The hosepipe is then connected to the pump.

The frame is laid on the pool bottom, and covered with well washed ¾ inch (19 mm) screened gravel, to a depth of approximately 18 inches (457 mm). The filter is then ready to operate. To be successful, the pump should be capable of producing a flow rate of not less than 110 gallons (454.5 litres) per hour, although, depending upon the size of the pool and number of fish, this may have to be considerably

Fig. 4.3 Filters

Top: Internal filter constructed with plastic pipes, to be placed in pool beneath layer of gravel
Bottom: Outside filter. Watertight compartments containing filter material, through which water passes before being returned to pool via the waterfall

increased. It would do no harm if the pump were powerful enough to turn the full gallonage of water over once in ever two hours!

External filters are usually employed in the filtration of large bodies of water. Watertight containers are erected above the level of the pool. In general, there are three or four containers each having internal measurements of approximately that of a 30 inch (762 mm) cube. From near the top of each compartment a large diameter plastic pipe leads nearly to the bottom of the adjoining compartment, allowing water to enter low down in the filter, and be discharged at the top of the next. Each container is filled with well washed coke, which is graded from large pieces in the first filter compartment to smaller pieces in the last container.

A powerful pump, with a flow rate of around 2000 gallons (9092 litres), is used to lift water to the filters. From the lower side of the first compartment, a pipe projects to connect, via a hosepipe, with the pump. Water is forced into the first filter and up through the bed of the coke, from there being discharged into the next filter, and so on, until it leaves the last container to re-enter the pool.

Both filter systems can be arranged to discharge down a waterfall, which will be beneficial by the resulting aeration of the filtered water. As both the internal and external filters rely upon the action of bacteria to be really effective, it will take some weeks for the colonies to become established. Therefore, because filtration builds up gradually, there will not be any immediately apparent difference in the water quality.

A pump capable of continuous operation must be used in both filtration methods; if the filters stop running, through the pump failing or being switched off, the colony of bacteria will die and the efficiency of the filters suffer. If this should happen it will be necessary to backflush the system, before setting it back into operation. Occasionally both types of filters should be back-flushed to remove accumulated debris and sediment. This action will not interfere with the well-being of the essential bacteria.

FOUNTAINS AND WATERFALLS

It must be said that: "**The only place for a fountain is in the formal pond.**" Fountains are an obvious work of man; an artificiality that does not blend with, nor occur in, nature. Even in the strictly formal setting the fountain is not recommended because water lilies are not happy in the company of a fountain — they dislike the disturbance of the water created by the device. It will be found that in warm dry weather the level of the pool may fall quite rapidly, due to the high rate of evaporation which the spray from a fountain encourages. Nevertheless, for those who find the attraction of the fountain too hard to resist, a little guidance might be welcomed.

Fountain effects can be produced in a variety of patterns, depending upon the types and number of heads being used. The height of the throw is dependent upon the capacity of the pump. The easiest type of fountain unit to install is the self-contained, submersible, electrically operated pump. Normally these pumps will throw a fountain pattern to a height of around 6 feet (1.83 m), which can usually be adjusted by a built-in flow regulator. At this height the approximate spread of the fall would be in a radius of 4 feet (1.22 m) and this should be taken into account when positioning the fountain in the pool. A variety of fountain heads are normally available for attachment to the pump. In practice, the pump is placed in the pool, possibly being raised on bricks, at such a height that the fountain head nozzle is just above the water surface.

It is also possible, in the formal pool, to have a fountain and statuary combined as a centre piece. These and ornamental wall fountains are generally available from water garden centres.

WATERFALLS

The informal type of pool, with a rockery background, invites a waterfall. Such a feature is far more in keeping with nature, and is beneficial to the pool inhabitants. A waterfall presents a greater body of water to the atmosphere due to its tumbling, cascading action, allowing it to be well oxygenated and to assist in the escape of odorous gases.

However complex or simple the design of the waterfall may be, it must conform to nature and be in harmony with its surroundings — a straight flight of steps is man's idea of a waterfall, not that of nature. Consider those pools in hilly or mountainous areas where water trickles down the hillsides from one pool to the next, tumbling and gurgling over the rocks, and try to create on a smaller scale a near imitation of the design perfected by Dame Nature.

The course of the waterfall may be laid with butyl pool liner sheet, creating depressions and waterways in one piece to avoid any leakage, leaving a flap to be hidden beneath rocks and plants. It can then be disguised by having rock carefully positioned in and around it, being sure not to obstruct the flow of water, and so causing it to flood into the surrounding area.

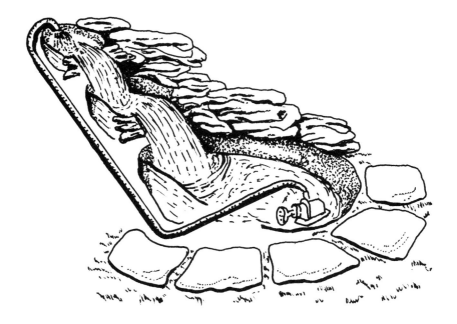

Fig. 4.4   Waterfall Installation
Pipework, carrying water to the waterfall head, should be buried, or hidden by some other means, to preserve the impression of a natural waterway. For the same reason the edges of the artificial water-course should be disguished by rocks or low-growing plants.

Concrete may also be used, mixed in the same proportions as used in the construction of the concrete pool. First line the course with polythene, to avoid water loss in the event of frost cracking the concrete at some future time, and shape the concrete course of the waterfall over this. Allow a thickness of around 4 inches (102 mm), and do not place any rocks in place until the concrete has hardened. Rockwork can then be cemented into position to give the appearance of a rocky water-course. Be careful not to impede the flow and thus cause an overflow on to the surrounding land. This type of construction must, of course, be rendered safe. It is best, therefore, to build the waterfall immediately after completion of the pool. If the waterfall is then allowed to operate continuously during the time that the pool is being cured, both pool and waterfall will be rendered safe and free of alkali simultaneously.

Preformed basins and courses are available, manufactured in glassfibre and other plastic materials, in a wide variety of shapes and textures. Choose a type with a natural coloured finish. They are installed in a stepped fashion so that water from each basin overflows into the one below. All that is required is to set them firmly in the ground, making sure that each is level and in the correct position to receive water from the one above. As these are made from moulds it is necessary to use some ingenuity to disguise them. It should be possible to hide their edges by the use of plants and overhanging rocks.

Whatever method of construction is used, the course of the waterfall must have side walls of sufficient height to contain the water; too flat or shallow and the water will overflow and escape. Water is lifted to the head of the waterfall by an electric pump, or received from a main water supply through plastic pipework. The pipes should be of sufficiently large bore and should run as straight as possible for the shortest feasible distance. Too many bends in a long run of pipework which has a bore that is too restrictive will cause friction that will slow the flow by its braking effect.

RILLS

A rill can be an attractive feature, especially if flanked by low rockeries. It is a very shallow water-course filled with stones and pebbles, through which water splashes and merrily gurgles on its way.

Use the soil from the pool to make the rockery if there's no natural bank or slope. Cut out the watercourse making steps as required. Any length of waterfall and stream can be made and a rock pool incorporated at the head if required.

The stones on the face should be set slightly higher to retain water in the channel when the pump is not running. The stones on the face will determine the flow of water — a flat stone will give a sheet of water whereas an arrangement of rockstone or cobbles will give a rippling rapid type cascade effect.

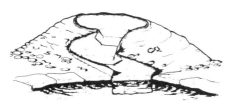

Lay the liner into the excavated watercourse. A single piece of liner can be used or several pieces which must be overlapped on the face of each waterfall ensuring the lower liner is higher than the water level on the overlap. Allow extra length for each fall to allow the material to be lifted to form the sides.

Lay the waterfall tubing and bury in the ground avoiding any sharp bends which may restrict the flow from the pump. Complete the remainder of the rockery and plant as required.

Starting at the bottom of the waterfall, lay the stones to the sides of the watercourse taking care to ensure the liner is set higher than the proposed water level. Gradually work up the watercourse at the same time constructing the face of each fall.

Install the pump as recommended by the manufacturers.

Fig. 4.5 Constructing a Waterfall
(Courtesy of Stapeley Water Gardens Ltd)

FILLING WITH WATER

When the planting of the pool, stream, marginal areas and bog garden has been completed, water must be introduced. It is at this stage that eagerness can only too easily over-ride patience. Hurried, unthinking action can quickly undo all the care that has been taken, as rushing water jets through the hosepipe, causing plants to be uprooted and the compost to be washed up in a great dirty cloud of mud.

The only safe way to go about introducing the water is as follows:

1. As the plants are put into place, cover them with sheets of wet newspaper to prevent them drying out. Cover all exposed compost in the same manner.

2. Place a large, shallow pan in the centre of the pool bottom and lead the hose into it, holding it in place with a weight of some sort.

3. Arrange for someone to turn on the water supply, while you watch the hose, and signal as soon as the water is flowing slowly and gently. The pond can then be left to fill very slowly to the required depth. The pan and weight can be removed when the water reaches a depth of about 12 inches (305 mm).

4. As the water level rises the newspaper will float free. It can then be carefully removed, taking care not to disturb the plants.

5. When the pool is successfully filled, leave everything to settle down for a few weeks to allow the plants to root firmly. It will then be ready for stocking with fish.

WATER BOARD REGULATIONS

In the construction of even the smallest water garden a large amount of water will be required. In recent years water has become a valuable and expensive commodity, and water which is drawn from the mains must be paid for. Those who can make use of a natural water supply are more fortunate than those who do not have such a luxury. However, **if a stream is to be diverted, the land-owners who have riparian rights, both upstream and down, should be informed and their consent sought.** Nothing is more calculated to upset neighbours than suffering a sudden drought or flood due to a temporary damming of the water course, and care should be taken to avoid such a mishap.

Those who are forced to rely upon mains water should contact their

**Large scale waterfall, streams
and canals are easily designed
and constructed with liners**

Fig. 4.6 Constructing Waterfalls and Canals
(Courtesy of Stapeley Water Gardens Ltd)

local Water Board, and seek their advice before installing any pipe or fitting which is connected to the water mains supply system; most Boards levy a charge for the use of a hosepipe, and for pools. They may calculate an annual charge, or insist upon installing a water meter. Normally an inspector will visit the applicant, both to advise and assess, and he will require that his Board's regulations are complied with.

Many, if not all, Water Boards will require that any hose or other pipe which is permanently connected to the main shall have an approved non-return valve fitted. Generally it is also stipulated that the ends of such pipes shall be positioned well above the water level of any pool or other body of water. Failure to comply with the Water Authority bye-laws and regulations can result in prosecution and, possibly, a heavy fine.

Most Water Board inspectors will be found very helpful, and there is nothing to fear when seeking their assistance in ensuring that everything has been done or is being done, in a correct and legitimate manner.

Fig. 5.1 Plants for the Water Garden
Top left: *Typha lattifolia*
Top right: *Caltha palustris*
Bottom left: *Hottonia palustris*
Bottom right: *Calla palustris*

Chapter 5

PLANTS FOR POOL AND BOG

PREPARATION

Plants in the pool may be grown either in a permanent position or in containers, the latter being a popular method which simplifies future maintenance. Suitable containers can be purchased from aquatic nurseries or water garden centres. The most suitable compost for the pool and waterside areas is a good turfy loam — the top spit from meadow-land would be ideal, providing that it has not been treated with any form of insecticide or weed-killing chemicals. It is not necessary to add any fertilizer although, if desired, a little bone-meal can be added. Place the loam where it is required, and lightly firm down, then cover with a 2 inch (51 mm) layer of well washed gravel or stone chippings, to prevent the fish stirring the muddy loam into the water. Finally, give a thorough soaking before inserting the plants.

SELECTION OF PLANTS

No gardener would knowingly introduce disease or pests to the garden, but this can happen all too easily in the case of water plants. Infectious fish diseases, parasites and other pests, leeches and snails are just a few of the problems than can be unwittingly brought in with water and bog garden plants. Experienced water gardeners view all new acquisitions, be they plant or fish, with great suspicion, irrespective of their source, and take preventative measures accordingly.

Possibly one of the best places from which to purchase plants is a nursery that specialises in the cultivation of coldwater plants. If it is possible to make a personal visit, so much the better — the conditions under which they are grown can be seen. Failing that, obtain a catalogue and order through the post. Many nurseries issue excellent catalogues, illustrating plants and giving growing instructions.

Avoid, if possible, plants which have been raised in warm water, or appear yellowish, drawn and spindly. Ideally the plant should be sturdy and a good, healthy green, with a strong root system. Some submerged water plants are sold as cuttings. Early spring, from April to June, is generally considered the best time of the year to obtain and set out water plants.

TREATMENT

Having obtained the plants, carefully swill them to remove any soil and other matter. Carefully remove yellow and dead leaves, and at the same time clean up the roots. Pay particular attention to the removal of any hair-like (or other) traces of algae which, if overlooked, can grow at an alarming rate. With the thumb and forefinger, rub off any worm-like creatures, snails, snail eggs or other jelly-like matter, together with any other suspicious material which is not part of the plant. Once the plants are as clean as possible they must be sterilized, for it is surprising how many unwelcome pests and parasites will have escaped even the most careful scrutiny. Dissolve crystals of *potassium permanganate* in warm water and add this solution to the sterilization bath in sufficient quantity to turn the water a light pink colour. Totally immerse the plants and leave them to soak for two or three hours. Finally, wash them under clean running water, whilst making sure that all unwanted matter has been removed, before placing into a container of clean water ready for planting.

It may be thought that going to so much trouble is a waste of time. This is far from true; careful preparation of the plants will help to avoid future problems, such as leeches, which can prove exceedingly difficult to eradicate from a pool.

POOL PLANTS

Pride of place in most pools goes to the queen of water plants, the water-lily. Therefore, it will be dealt with first, in some detail, for it deserves lengthy consideration, as befits such a popular and regal plant.

The water-lily bears the title of *Nymphaea*, bestowed upon it by von Linné, and is steeped in history and tradition. The name *Nymphaea* is a direct transliteration of a Greek word which Theophrastus — a disciple of Plato and Aristotle — used when describing these plants some three hundred years before the birth of Christ, and refers to the early Greek practice of dedicating the water-lily to the nymphs.

Some 1700 years earlier, the Pharaohs and priests of Egypt were being laid to rest with wreathes made from the petals of the blue-flowered *Nymphaea caerulea*. The white-flowered Nymphaea lotus is known to have been cultivated by the Ancient Egyptians as long ago as 3000-2500 B.C., the flowers being used in their religious festivals.

Although the cosmopolitan Nymphacaea has been cultivated in various parts of the world for many years, it is of comparatively recent acquaintance to British gardeners.

Interest really awoke in 1849, when Mr. Paxton, gardener to the Duke of Devonshire, became the first person to flower the giant *Victoria amazonia*. This tropical water-lily was discovered in 1802 by the botanist Haenke in a backwater of the Bolivian Amazon.

JOSEPH LATOUR-MARLIAC

American horticulturists have produced many beautiful hybrids, but none can compare to those of the Frenchman, Joseph Latour-Marliac. In 1858 only the white-flowered *N. alba* was commonly available for outside cultivation, and Marliac decided to attempt to produce more colourful hardy water-lilies.

Marliac commenced by collecting different species from various parts of the world, and then began a programme of breeding. He spent several years producing and flowering hundreds of seedlings, with very little success. However, in 1879, he evolved *N. X. marliacea rosea,* and from that stage new varieties were produced thick and fast. Over seventy new varieties were developed and most were more than successful.

During his lifetime Marliac introduced many spectacular hybrids — a legacy that the present-day gardener still enjoys. He died in 1911, taking his closely guarded secrets with him. Amongst the hybrids developed by this genius are plants suited to waters of shallow depth and to waters of considerable depth. He honoured his son-in-law, Maurice Laydeker, by naming *Laydekeri* hybrids after him.

Most specialist water-lily nurseries produce illustrated catalogues, which are well worth obtaining. These not only illustrate the various varieties of water-lily which the nursery can offer, but indicate the depth of water best suited to each and often instructions on their cultivation. Many of the water-lilies which are intended for deeper water will also succeed in shallower depths — although they may tend to overpower the smaller pool — whereas those which require shallow water will be unlikely to do well if planted in water which is too deep. The following is no more than a list of the more popular types which are generally available, and is given to indicate the wide choice available.

Attraction. A popular red variety — the flower passes through rich crimson to deep red.

Fig. 5.2 Plants for the Water Garden
Top left: *Sagittaria sagittifolia*
Top right: *Iris pseudacorus*
Bottom left: *Aponogeton distachyus*
Bottom right: *Nymphaecae (water lily)*
Bottom centre: *Nuphar lutea (brandy bottle)*

Graziella. Reddish-copper flowers turning to orange-yellow.

Froebelii. An ideal water-lily for the smaller pool. Bright red flowers.

Laydekeri lilacea. Another plant suitable for shallow water, it has pink flowers.

Gladstonia. Large pure white flowers with rich golden stamens.

Pygmaea helvola. Small, with yellow flowers.

Escarboucle. Very prolific with large red flowers which mature to a rich crimson colour.

James Brydon. A lighter red with cup-shaped flowers and purple leaves.

Esmerelda. Rose-white, mottled and striped deep rose.

Sultan. Cherry-red, stained white.

Sunrise. Fragrant, huge, sunshine-yellow flowers.

Rose Arey. Strongly perfumed, subtle reddish-pink blossoms with sharply pointed, incurved petals.

Marliacea chromatella. Cup-shaped golden-yellow flower which lifts out of the water.

Marliacea rosea. A very hardy variety, it has almost white flowers which gradually take on a pinkish sheen.

Marlicaea albida. White flowers with a pinkish bloom. A suitable variety for shallowish water.

Odorata sulphurea grandiflora. Yellow, star-shaped flowers.

Tuberosa richardsoni. A strong growing, deep water variety. It has sparkling white flowers.

Nymphaea alba. White flowers. Common water-lily, native to many British waters.

Prior to planting the water-lily, all dead leaves and stems should be removed and the roots trimmed. They must be cleaned and sterilized.

The *Odorata* and *Tuberosa* types have long fleshy rhizomes which should be set under an inch (2.5 cm) of the planting medium leaving the crown exposed. Tubers of the *Marliacea* group are large and rounded with fibrous roots. These should be planted vertically with the roots well spread out and the crown above the compost. The *Laydekeri* group have a similar, but smaller, rootstock to the *Marliacea* and are best set in a semi-horizontal position with the crown exposed.

PLANTING

Planting is best carried out between May and June, when the plant is starting into growth. Water-lilies can be planted in containers or directly into the pool. Container planting is the better method for the average pool because it allows easy removal for periodic trimming or division. After planting, the water-lily should be held in place with a weight, to prevent if floating free when submersed in the pool. After planting it should be either lowered gradually to the bottom of the pool, over a period of time, or covered with around 6 inches (152 mm) of water. As the water-lily grows, slowly increase the water depth so that the growth remains just below the water surface, until the correct water level is reached.

Propagation is by division of the rootstock during April and May. A sharp knife should be used to cut the tough rhizomes. Each crown is left with several inches of the tuber attached and the severed sections are then planted in the normal way.

The Water Hawthorn *(Aponogeton distachyus)* has a similar mode of growth to the water-lily, and is also worthy of inclusion in the pool, if only for its sweet, vanilla-like perfume that scents the evening air so delightfully. Originating from the South African Cape of Good Hope, it has long been established in cooler climates. The elongated, ovoid-shaped leaves float upon the water surface and are green, becoming mottled with purplish-brown blotches. A forked spike carries the flower, which is snowy-white with black anthers, above the surface of the water. Seed is formed quite readily and young seedlings may be found floating in the pool — they appear rather like small fine-stemmed grass. These may be inserted into the pool compost, where they will grow on. This plant is cultivated in the same manner as the water-lily, and will grow in water from 6 inches (152 mm) to 2 feet (610 mm) deep.

Other submerged plants for the pool or stream are:

Elodea canadensis. An excellent oxygenator that consists of a much branched number of stems, thickly dressed in narrow leaves. It is a fast growing plant if conditions suit it. Sold as cuttings, it will root quite easily.

Elodea densa is similar to, but stouter than, the previous plant. The main stems are sparsely branched and the narrow leaves grow in whorls around the stem. It is also sold as cuttings.

Lagarosiphon muscoides. Very similar to *E. densa;* it is distinctly tubular in appearance. The branched stem is thick, but tends to be brittle, and is encircled by dark-green, crispate leaves. Sold and grown in the same manner as the *Elodeas.*

Ceratophyllum demersum (Hornwort). Has a seasonal cycle and dies back over the winter period. This plant has the curious habit of not developing roots, although it will often develop a light-coloured shoot that will anchor it to the growing medium. It is many-branched, dark green and stiffish, the older portion becoming bare of leaves. The leaves are needle-like in appearance and arranged in whorls around the stem. They are very brittle and the plant should be handled with care. Weight the plant down to prevent if floating to the water surface.

Myriophyllum spicatum and *M. verticillatum* are more commonly known as **Milfoils.** Although they appear very similar to the previous plant they are, in fact, much sturdier and develop strong root systems. Sold as cuttings, they are easy to propagate.

Callitriche palustris is easily propagated from cuttings and is fast growing. The plant has both underwater leaves, and rosettes of surface-floating leaves. Often seen in natural streams.

Ranunculus aquatilis **(Water crowfoot).** Bears white flowers with a yellow patch at the base, borne on upright stalks which hold the flowers above the water surface. The submerged leaves are finely divided into stiff, hair-like segments; the floating leaves, however, are kidney-shaped, divided into three lobes and three leaflets. Roots easily from cuttings.

Hottonia palustris **(Water violet).** Another flowering plant, it bears lilac-tinted spikes of flowers some 8-10 inches (203-254 mm) above the water. The fern-like leaves grow alternatively upon branched stems. Propagate by division of the rootstock. Each cutting must carry some roots.

When calculating the number of submerged plants required, allow approximately twenty to twenty-four plants for every square foot of the bottom area.

MARGINAL PLANTS

Marginal plants are suitable for planting in shallow water and the bog garden. They require cleaning and sterilizing with the same care as the other water plants.

Do not attempt to grow too many different kinds of marginal plants, or the effect will be lost. A few grouped together, as in nature will look far more pleasing. By the same token, select plants which are in keeping with the size of the pool. A small pool surrounded by some of the larger marginal plants will look completely wrong, and small plants around a large pool would seem very insignificant. If possible, choose plants with different flowering periods, to extend the season for as long as possible.

Planting must be firm — if necessary weight the plants until the roots have taken hold, and do not plant deeper than the pale bottom portions of the plant, which give a clue to the depth at which it was previously growing. Plant between April and June.

The following plants should be suitable for growing in about 6 inches (152 mm) of water and be equally at home in the marshy conditions of the bog-garden, or any situation in between.

Acorus calamus (**Sweet Flag**). Grows to 3 feet (915 mm). Scented. Small yellowish flowers during June-July.

Butomus umbellatus (**Flowering Rush**). Height 2-4 feet (610-915 mm). Sword-shaped leaves. Umbrellas of small rose-pink flowers during June-August.

Calla palustris (**Bog Arum**). Height 6-9 inches (152-229 mm). Heart-shaped leaves. Creeping rootstock. White arum-like flowers April-June.

Caltha palustris (**Marsh marigold**). Grows to 1 foot (305 mm) and prefers moist conditions, rather than being under water. Heart-shaped leaves. Butter-yellow flowers during April-May. Cultivated varieties are *alba*, 8 inches (203 mm), single white flowers; *nana plena*, 8 inches (203 mm). double-flowered; *plena*, up to 15 inches (381 mm), double golden-yellow flowers; *polypetala*, height 2-3 feet (610-915 mm), large leaves and yellow flowers up to 3 inches across (76 mm), during spring.

Glyceria spectabilis. Height up to 3 feet (915 mm). Striped, rush-like leaves with green, white and yellow colours, developing a reddish tint late in the season.

Iris laevigata. Height 2 feet (610 mm). Sword-shaped leaves. Blue flowers June-September. *I. laevigata atropururea:* violet flowers; the *alba* variety has white flowers.

Iris kaempferi. Flowers in a range of colours from white to blue and red. Prefers moist conditions.

Iris versicolour. Height 15-18 inches (381-457 mm). Red and blue flowers marked with yellow.

Iris pseudacorus. Grows to 3 feet (915 mm). *Alba* has white flowers; *bastardii*, primrose flowers; *variegata*, yellow flowers.

Juncus effusus spiralis (**Corkscrew Rush**). 18 inches (457 mm) corkscrew twisted stems; *vittatus* has 3 feet (915 mm) high leaves striped yellow.

Mentha aquatica (**Water mint**). Height 1-4 feet (305-1219 mm), lilac flowers during August and September.

Mimulus lutens (**Monkey Musk**) Height 18 inches (457 mm), the flowers are golden-yellow spotted red and are produced all summer long. *M. ringens* has blue flowers and grows to 15 inches (381 mm). There are a number of other cultivated varieties, some with reddish flowers.

Myosotis scorpioides (**Forget-me-not**). Height 9-12 inches (229-305 mm). Sky-blue flowers May-July. Must be controlled.

Saururus cernuus (**Swamp Lily**) Height 1 to 2 feet (305-610 mm), heart-shaped leaves, dark green and up to 6 inches (152 mm) long. The flowers are white and fragrant during Summer.

Scirpus albescens. This rush grows to 3 feet (915 mm), the stems being variegated green and white. *S. cernuus* (syn *Isolepis gracilis*). A tufted rush growing to height of 6-12 inches (152-305 mm), with drooping stems. this family includes, amongst other, the Bulrush — *S. lacustris* — which reaches a height of 6 feet (1829 mm).

Typha minima. A small reedmace with rusty brown pistillates, growing to 1½ feet (457 mm).

The following plants prefer a position that allows them to have around 3 inches (76 mm) of water over their growing point:

Alisma plantago-aquatica (**Great Water Plantain**). 2-3 feet (610-915 mm). Rose coloured flowers.

Glyceria aquatica (**Reed Manna Grass**). Height 4-6 feet (1219-1829 mm).

Glyceria aquatica variegata. Height 18-24 inches (457-610 mm). White, yellow and green striped foliage.

Iris pseudacorus (**Yellow Water Flag**). Grows 3-5 feet (915-1524 mm) and bears golden yellow flowers.

Pontederia cordata (**Pickerel Weed**). Height 2 feet (610 mm). Arrow-shaped leaves top the stems. Spikes of blue flowers during Summer.

Sagittaria macrophylla. Height 3 feet (915 mm). White mid-summer flowers.

Sagittaria sagittifolia (**Common Arrowhead**). Height 18 inches (457 mm). White flowers during mid-Summer.

Sagittaria sagittifolia japonica. Height 2½ feet (762 mm) with white double flowers during mid-summer.

The *Sagittarias* will thrust up from a depth of 12 inches (305 mm) or more, some producing underwater foliage as well as the arrow-shaped above-water leaf.

Typha lattifolia (**Great Reed Mace**). Grows to a height of up to 8 feet (2438 mm). Dark chocolate-brown pistillates.

The foregoing plants are but a few of the many which are available, and a water-plant nursery catalogue should be consulted for a greater selection.

Apart from occasionally thinning to prevent any plant trying to over-run a weaker neighbour, these plants only need cutting down to remove dead foliage during the winter in order to keep them tidy.

Chapter 6

STOCKING THE WATER

Having laid the pools and other water features, to which the various plants have been added, it can be said that the essential backbone of the water garden has been constructed. However attractive it may be, creating a truly attractive feature requires more than plants alone. In order to complete the water-life picture it is necessary to include fish, which will add the undeniable interest of below water life to the scene.

SELECTING HEALTHY FISH

Careful attention should be given to the selection of any fish which is to be purchased. Stock offered by aquatic-pet shops, water-garden nurseries and other dealers are, almost without exception, imported. Such fishes will usually be suffering from the stress caused by a great deal of handling, a long air-journey and changes in climate and water conditions. Such fish will be weakened, and susceptible to a host of maladies. However, careful observation and a sharp eye can help to reduce to some degree the risk of buying a sick or ailing fish. If there is even the slightest doubt, it is much the safest policy to resist temptation rather than risk buying a suspect fish, which may not have long to live. Patience and discretion will lessen the risk of wasting money on worthless, unhealthy stock. Much can be learned from first impressions when entering a dealer's premises. The attitude of the vendor, and the cleanliness of the premises, will clearly indicate whether to venture further or beat a hasty retreat.

POINTS TO LOOK FOR

A close inspection of pools or tanks will reveal whether the dealer is concerned for the welfare of the stock. Pools and tanks should be reasonably spacious, with no undue overcrowding of the fish. The fish should be active, not sulking, and there should not be any dead fish in evidence. If all seems well, greater attention can be paid to the condition of the fish. They should be swimming in an easy, balanced manner without any difficulty or jerkiness. The eyes should be clear and bright with no trace of a cloudy, whitish film. The fins, held erect and well spread, should be free of any milkiness or blood streaks. the body must appear to be well nourished and have no sign of injury or disease.

A wasted body that makes the head appear too large; dull, cloudy eyes, or eyes covered by a whitish film; split or torn, ragged, fins; blood spots or streaks upon the body or fins; a greyish-white bloom or film that partially obscures the colour on any part of the body or head; scales that seem to be raised instead of lying flat; any traces of small white 'cotton-wool' tufts of fungus, any minute white spots, pimples, ulcers, or holes, and apparent pieces of 'thread' anywhere on the fish — these are all positive signs of future trouble and such fish must be avoided, together with any seemingly healthy fish that occupy the same water. The same may be said for any fish which makes sudden wild dashes, rubbing itself against any firm surface, or has difficulty swimming in a normal fashion. Be cautious at all times, especially when considering the purchase of imported stock. Be safe rather than sorry — far better to swallow your eagerness and go away empty-handed to try elsewhere.

Although most dealers in pet fish put the fish into a plastic bag in which the buyer can carry it home, there is always the possibility of an accident. It is therefore a wise precaution to have a lidded plastic bucket with you when buying fish — the lid will prevent any water splashing out during the journey home. In this way the fish can be transported quite long distances safely, with no risk of any leakage. The alternative is to carry a strong, watertight plastic bag into which the dealer's bag can be placed. However, the bucket is definitely the better method.

TYPES OF FISH

The *Cyprinidae,* or Carp family, provides species most suitable for stocking the man-made pools of the water garden. One of the characteristics of this family is that they have no teeth. They are therefore quite harmless. Due to their harmless nature, different species will peacefully share the same water, provided that none is so small that another may be tempted into eating it for, as mentioned earlier, they are cannibalistic by nature. All are omnivorous and thus present no feeding difficulties. Their breeding patterns follow closely those described for the goldfish, and each lays demersal eggs which fall through the water to adhere to water plants. The following are all members of the *Cyprinidae.*

The goldfish has for many years been the most popular choice of fish for the ornamental pool. There are a number of reasons why this should be so: it adapts well to most conditions in which it is kept; it is not finicky about its food; it is long-lived and, being tenacious of life, can live for around twenty years in the correct environment; it does not grow too large to manage, reaching a body length of something in the region of twelve inches (305 mm) under good conditions, and, as everyone must know, has a most splendid colour.

The goldfish is so well-known that it needs no description, but how many of its admirers are aware that it has a recorded history which spans a period of around 1000 years? This long pedigree has been well recorded from its early days in China to recent times.

The native Chinese carp, a dull greenish-olive species, has a marked tendency to produce fish with a yellow colour and from such specimens the well-known goldfish was produced. By selective breeding and other means the ancient Chinese not only improved the colour and form, but they also created a number of fancy varieties that had scant resemblance to their original wild forebears.

VARIETIES OF GOLDFISH

Of the many goldfish varieties, some of which were developed in Japan from Chinese stock, only the following can be said to be suitable for outside pool accommodation:

Common Goldfish *(Carassius auratus)*. A good specimen will have a well-proportioned, sturdy look about it, with a moderately curved back and corresponding curve to the underside of the body. The head should be short and wide, with a smallish mouth and bright eyes.

The scales have a shining metallic appearance and cover the whole body, with the exception of the head and fins. Single-coloured reddish-orange, orange or yellow are generally preferred to the variegated types. However, reddish-orange and yellow, red and silvery-white, or yellow and silvery-white are not uncommon. Black may also be exhibited, but this is not a permanent colour and will slowly disappear over a period of time. Pure silvery-white fish are not highly thought of by fish-keeping enthusiasts. For this reason, those fish which display any silvery-white colour are often avoided, since the colour has a tendency to gradually spread.

Comet *(Carassius auratus var)*, is somewhat slimmer than the common goldfish, but carries the same type of scales and colours. It does, however, have longer, more developed fins. Most noticeable is the tail — this is as long as the body of the fish, and very deeply forked. It has a very streamlined look about it, and is capable of quite a fast

Fig. 6.1 Fish for the Pool
1 Common goldfish 2 Bristol shubunkin 3 Comet 4 Tench 5 Koi 6 Crucian carp 7 Orfe 8 Minnow

turn of speed when the occasion demands it.

London Shubunkin *(Carassius auratus var)*. This variety is almost indentical to the common goldfish, the essential different being the colour. This fish lacks the reflective tissue and metallic shine, the thin transparent scales allowing a multiplicity of colours to be seen. Ideally the background colour should be a bright, forget-me-not blue, although slate-blue is very common and not highly prized. Over the background are splashed patches of red, yellow, brown, violet and black, over which there is black speckling. The colours should spread into the fins. Fish that are a single self-colour, or whitish-pink, are not considered to be of any value.

Bristol Shubunkin *(Carassius auratus var)*. This variety of goldfish was developed by early members of the Bristol Aquarists Society, and is very popular and attractive. The colour is exactly the same as described for the London Shubunkin. The body is streamlined and slim. All fins are very well-developed, the dorsal fin being as high as the body is deep. The tail, which is the feature of this fish, is large and well developed, being well-spread with no sign of drooping. The lobes are large and rounded. All other fins are equally well-developed and longish.

BREEDING

The goldfish, and its varieties, will interbreed unless kept separated. During spawning the fish become oblivious to all dangers as the males pursue the females in a wild chase in and around the underwater plants. Eggs are fertilized and released in an indiscriminate manner as they fall through the water. The time it takes for the eggs to hatch depends very much upon the water temperature — the warmer the water the quicker the hatching time. The eggs are roughly the size of a pin-head and a translucent clear to amber colour. Infertile eggs turn white and become fungused.

Upon hatching, the tiny fish are approximately 1/5 inch (5 mm) long, and look like small glass splinters as they rest amongst the plants. Those which survive the attentions of the adult fish should grow to a length of about 2 inches (50 mm) by the end of the season, and should have assumed their adult colours. Goldfish during the early days of their life are a greenish-olive colour. However, this slowly changes to the essential colours required of its particular variety. Any fish which has failed to change colour by the end of the season must be removed. If allowed to remain, these wild-coloured fish will eventually breed and produce an ever increasing number of similar fish. It they are allowed to continue breeding it wll be to the definite detriment of the better coloured specimens.

Apart from the goldfish there is only one other member of the genus *Carassius* — the Crucian carp. This and other members of the *Cyprinidae* (Carp family) are now described.

Crucian Carp *(Carassius carassius)*, or bronze carp, as it is sometimes called, is a close relative of the goldfish. It has a somewhat similar body shape and fins, but does not possess the bright colours of the goldfish, nor does it usually grow quite so large. In general the colour of the Crucian carp is dull bronze, olive or greenish-olive, with a brassy-yellow belly. It has the same spawning habits as the goldfish, and its average lifespan is around seven years.

Common Carp *(Cyprinus carpio)*. Unlike goldfish and Crucian carp, these fish have four barbels on the upper lip. They can reach a length of two feet (610 mm) or more, and have an elongated body. The back is blue-green to brownish-green, and the sides bluish-green to golden-yellow, whilst the fins are bluish-green tinged with red. There are a number of varieties of this carp, all being quite hardy in the outdoor pool.

Mirror Carp *(Cyprinus carpio var)*. This variety has been produced by selective breeding, and differs from the Common carp only in its scale covering. This variety lacks most of its scales, but those which it does possess are large, with a metallic lustre, and are mostly along the lateral line and at the base of the fins.

Leather Carp *(Cyprinus carpio var)*. This is almost entirely without scales, the skin having a leathery look.

Koi *(Cyprinus carpio var)*. During recent years this has become a very popular fish for the large pool, and has attracted a great many devotees.

THE KOI CARP

This variety was originally developed in Japan, which still produces the finest specimens. Originally introduced into Japan as food fish, the Japanese noted occasional colour mutations that differed from those of the Common carp. These were segregated and selectively bred to enhance the coloration of what then became domestic pets. At the Grand Exhibition of 1914, held in Tokyo's Ueno Park, these fish drew large crowds when they were exhibited. So great was the interest that professional fish breeders began to breed and cultivate the fish, some producing remarkable examples of improved colours. From Japan, the Koi has slowly spread to many parts of the world.

Koi are the largest domesticated ornamental fish, reaching a length of 24 inches (610 mm) or more when kept under ideal conditions. Due to their size, and habit of grubbing in the sediment and plant compost for food, it is almost impossible to grow any but the strongest rooting plants in their pool. Many Koi keepers rely upon filtration to preserve the water clarity, and on water-lilies for ornamentation.

Whilst all Koi are of the same species, *Cyprinus carpio,* they are, nevertheless, arranged into various varieties which are given Japanese names. These names are given to fish with certain colours and patterns, and are generally descriptive of those patterns — if one understands Japanese. Unfortunately, for the most part, these different varieties do not breed true. Possibly the most popular variety of Koi is that known as the **Kōhaku,** which is a white fish overlaid with a red pattern. the **Shūsui** is an old variety developed by Kichigorö Akiyama Sr., between 1868 and 1926. It has mirror-like scales and the back is sky-blue, becoming lighter on the sides, the lower sides being red.

Being bred for the pool, the colours of Koi tend to be at their most concentrated on the upper part of the body. They are therefore best viewed from above. A facet of these fish which endears them to many owners is the ease with which they are tameable and can be taught to feed from the hand.

OTHER TYPES OF FISH

Orfe *(Idus idus).* An admirable fish for the pool, for it is an active creature, spending much of its time near the water surface. It does, however, require cool, well-oxygentated water to be at its best. A large streamlined fish which can grow to around 20 inches (51 cm) or more, and is fairly fast growing. Generally, the back is greyish-black and the sides paler, with a silvery belly. The fins are reddish, except for the greyish tail and dorsal fin.

There is a particularly attractive golden variety, known as the **Golden Orfe,** which has a back of pale gold shading to pink suffused with silver on the belly.

On a warm summer day these fish will do much to keep down the nuisance of any winged insects which may approach the water surface, as the fast swimming Orfe leap to capture their prey, which seldon manages to escape.

Tench *(Tinca tinca).* The Green or Common Tench is useful for its habit of scavenging in the depths of the pool. However, due to this habit it is seldom seen. It is a sluggish fish, with a rounded appearance. The body is rather stout, with a rounded back and all of the fins are rounded, including the lobes of the tail. At both corners of the mouth is a small barbel. The very slimy body varies in colour from deep-olive to brownish-black, being a shade lighter on the belly. In the garden pool the fish grows to around 12 inches (305 mm) or less, and has a life of about seven years.

Golden Tench *(Tinca tinca var)*. A cultivated variety, bred specifically for the ornamental pool, it is a rich bronze colour.

Minnow *(Phoxinus phoxinus)*. An attractive, active little fish which seldom grows to more than 4 inches (102 mm). Ideally it should be kept in fair numbers, for the Minnow is gregarious by nature and prefers to swim in a shoal. When spawning, a shallow, stoney area is chosen and, at this time, its normal coloration becomes tinged with green and red.

Rudd *(Scardinius erythrophthalmus)*, or Common Rudd is a most attractive fish, which does well in the ornamental pool. Although the colour is variable, it is usually a brassy-green, shading to brassy-yellow on the sides, the belly being silvery-white. Generally, the fins are reddish, and the eyes brassy or golden. In length it averages 12 inches (305 mm), and can live for about five years. There are both silver and golden varieties bred for the ornamental pool.

Such fish as **Pike** *(Esox lucious)*, **Perch** *(Perca fluviatilis)*, **European Catfish** *(Silurus glanis)* and the **American Catfish** *(Ameriurus nebulosus)* are quite unsuited for inclusion in the ornamental pool. They are all very predatory by nature, and will readily eat any fish small enough to be taken.

TREATMENT OF NEWLY-ACQUIRED FISH

From whatever source new fish are obtained, they should be viewed with some suspicion. Fish caught in the wild are almost certain to be carrying parasites, whilst those purchased from a dealer could be carrying a latent disease. Such problems may not be readily obvious, but could become very obvious within a few days of their acquisition. The wise will take sensible steps to avoid, as far as possible, introducing any potentially ailing fish into the ornamental pond. The solution is to ensure that all new fish go through a period of quarantine, allowing sufficient time for any unsuspected troubles to manifest themselves. **This period should last for not less than twenty-eight days.**

Prior to obtaining the fish, prepare a container of suitable size by partially filling it with clean water. On arrival at their new home, the plastic bag (or whatever) in which the fish have been transported is floated, without unfastening it, in the previously prepared container. It is left for there two or three hours, to allow the two water temperatures to equalise. It then only remains to unfasten the container of fish, and allow them to swim free — do not pour them into the water.

During this period of quarantine, the fish should be fed sparingly, commencing with very small feeds and gradually increasing the amount offered. Usually fish purchased from a commercial source have been fed very frugally. Heavy feeding after a fast is exceedingly bad for the fish, as it is for most creatures. This period can also be used to give one or two precautionary disinfectant baths against parasites. **Sterazin,** a proprietary treatment available from most good dealers in pet-fish, is very effective if used according to the manufacturer's instructions.

If at the end of the period of quarantine the fish have proved to be healthy, they may be placed into the pool. To avoid chilling, float the fish in a container of the water in which they have been quarantined in the pool until the temperatures have equalised, then let them swim away.

There is little doubt about the best time of the year to buy fish. Spring means that the warmer days are ahead, and the warm months will encourage the fish to eat and put on growth. Little more can be said in respect of the fish; at the end of the day it is the common-sense, discretion, care and observation of the purchaser that will decide the health and quality of any newly-acquired fish.

This chapter cannot be completed, however, without advising that snails, and the like, **should not be placed into the pool or other water.** They can become a great nuisance and are of no benefit. They also eat the vegetation and the spawn of the fish. No gardener would knowingly introduce snails into the flower garden — why then should they be allowed in the water garden?

Chapter 7

ROCK FEATURES

The well-planned water garden nearly always makes use of rockwork, in the form of rockeries of one form or another. It may be incorporated as a background to a pool, with a watery cascade falling down its stoney face; it may be used along the banks of a stream, or as a retaining wall between different terrace levels. This popular feature can be of any size from a square yard to a square mile, only the scope of planting and treatment in the use of rock differing. In both instances, alpine plants can be grown with picturesque effect. However, to be successful the rocky features should be constructed with care and thought. To this end nature should be studied where, it will be noted, rocks are firmly planted in the ground and follows a definite stratum. Imitate nature, for there is no better teacher, and, above all, avoid putting the rockwork in regimental rows. Nature abhors straight lines, so give the rockwork an irregularity of line.

CHOOSING THE STONE

One of the problems which will have to be considered is the kind of stone to be used. When used near (or in) water, the choice is of the utmost importance. It must be hard and lime-free — the risk of alkali entering the water must be avoided for the safety of the fish. If a 'safe' local stone can be obtained it will obviously pay to do so; it will be found in most cases that this works out satisfactorily from an artistic point of view. Being quarried locally, it will probably be cheaper than stone which has to be brought in from some distance away and, being local, it is likely to be somewhat similar in nature to the soil of the locality. Plants which flourish in the ordinary soil of the gardens will find an equally happy home amongst the local rocks.

Always select rock of the largest manageable size, but bear in mind that each piece of stone will have to be man-handled into position, and while the back may ache it should not be broken. It should hardly need saying that the rock must all be of the same kind and, preferably, weather-worn in order to create a harmonious and natural-looking scene. Great height is not necessary — in fact it is seldom advisable to build a rockery higher than 3 feet (915 mm), otherwise it may over-power the pool and prove rather difficult to maintain.

PREPARING THE SITE

The first step in making a rockery is to decide roughly on the con-tour; that is to say, to decide whether it will be a rockery mound, a rocky slope, or merely outcrops of rock alongside a stream. It is possi-ble to create any of these quite simply, in quite small areas of garden.

Some excavation may be necessary to form the envisaged contour, and it should be remembered that the top spit of soil is the most fer-tile. The best plan is to strip off this fertile top spit, and to pile it in a heap at one side while the general outline of the rock garden is being built-up. The next step is to trench the soil all over the site, and to fill with at least a 6 inch (152 mm) depth of rubble (for example, builders bricks, broken concrete, stones, gravel and similar rough material). This will ensure good drainage over the site of the rock garden. The subsoil is then roughly rebuilt to the desired form, and well consoli-dated.

When possible, arrange the steepest slopes to be on the side of the rockery which will be in the shade, while the sunnier slopes are more gently sloped. If the slopes are arranged in this manner it will mean that those plants on the sunnier slope will suffer less from lack of moisture. It also allows a larger area of rockery pockets to enjoy full sunshine, and the majority of rock plants are sun lovers.

No rockery should be placed in perpetual shade, nor under drip-ping trees — hardly any of nature's rock gardens are found in such positions. Although there are enchanting rocky dells in deep crevices in hilly limestone districts, and some similar situations, but in such places the plantlife consists mostly of ferns and other foliage plants, and not the brightly coloured, flower-massed pockets beloved by the average rock gardener.

BUILDING THE ROCK GARDEN

The actual building of a rock garden is done from the bottom up-wards, and in the placing of the rocks the gardener reveals any artistic taste — or lack of it. Each stone must be selected with care and firmly placed into position. The stone should be set into the soil so that it is part buried and sits solidly upon a wide base. Each rock should be tilted backwards so that it leans into the slope. The reason for the tilt is to ensure that rain, as it falls, will travel into the rockery, where the plant roots are waiting for it, and not run to waste down the rock faces. Rocks so placed will form natural ledges and pockets to support the soil in which the plants are set. Nature's rock gardens are formed when stones have crashed down a mountain side and lodged in this position. Fine soil is washed down after them, filling the natural pockets which, after a time, become occupied by plants.

If there is a natural strata to the rocks, marked with parallel lines, they should be placed so that they are uniformly horizontal or sloping. Also, any weather-worn, lichen-covered portion, which has the most attractive appearance, should be allowed to be on the upper, exposed surface of the rock. This method of building will give the most natural appearance, so that the rockery will give the impression of being a natural and picturesque outcrop of stone.

MORAINES

In some situations it may be possible to construct a **moraine garden.** There are in nature two types of moraine: they are very similar to each other and differ mainly in the matter of age. As a glacier recedes it leaves in its wake a confused drift of stones, often piled in one place by the meeting of two glacier streams. At first these are partly covered by icy-cold water flowing from the glacier. Slowly, over a period of time, these stones, together with soil formed from softer material, are left high and dry, with no glacier water, but only the falling rain to sustain the plants which have taken root in the debris.

In Britain it is not possible to reproduce the conditions of the moraine described, where icy water trickles through the tumbled stones. However, it is possible to imitate the other moraine where most of the water has gone and the surface stones are dry at all times. An easy way to reproduce moraine conditions is to use a south-facing bank with a gradient of not more than one in ten — if water oozes naturally from the bank, so much the better. A large quantity of small stones, preferably water-worn and weathered, plus plenty of grit and a little soil, are needed for building.

With a little ingenuity a moraine can be contrived to top a rockery, which would be an advantage for this type of garden. Its position above the ordinary garden level would ensure that the moraine was well-drained, and the moraine plants would be less liable to suffer from surface damp. If at the same time a subterranean trickle of water can be arranged to pass under the artificial moraine and escape to form a cascade down the rockery, a fairly cool root run will be sec-

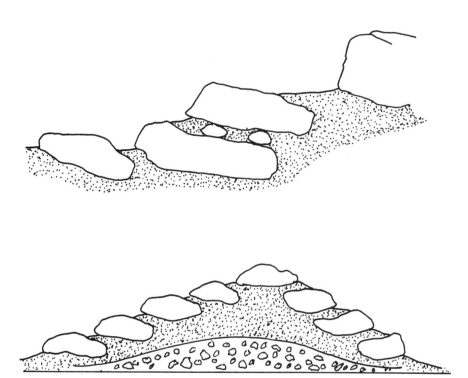

Fig. 7.1   Rockery Construction
Top: Stones should be tilted backwards, to allow moisture to run into the soil, and they must be firmly bedded. By placing small stones between large rocks the two are kept apart
Bottom: Build the rockery over a foundation of rubble to ensure good drainage

ured. This will give the nearest possible imitation of a natural moraine within the compass of the average garden.

CONSTRUCTION

Line a shallow depression, as described in an earlier chapter, to render it waterproof, with a discharge to the head of the cascade. Layer the depression with coarse sand at the bottom, adding stones and grit to create a mound, and mix a little fibrous loam with the grit as the work is carried out. It is then ready for planting, and the cascade water will appear to originate from an underground spring.

As mentioned earlier, a rockery can take the form of a **wall garden,** which acts as a retaining wall between different levels. This is constructed in the same way that the more usual type of rockery is built, by bedding the stone in layered stratas to the required height.

Dry walling is another method of retaining two different terrace levels. This will give a much more harmonious and natural look to the water garden, especially when the crevices are filled with plants, than a blank, cold stone wall with mortar-filled joints.

It is most important that a dry wall should not be vertical, but inclined backwards, with a slope of about 1 in 5, and care should be taken that the stones are set with a backwards slope, so that rain will run to the plant roots.

Artificial stone and cement blocks can be used, but the better result is obtained by using natural, stratified rocks, which can be split into slabs of various sizes and thicknesses, and can be easily handled. If the stones are not of suitable shape they can then be roughly hewn with a hammer to the desired length or thickness, before being laid. Low dry walls can be erected directly on the ground, or slightly sunken, or, to ensure stability and prevent sinking, the higher walls should be built up from a concrete foundation. As the work of building proceeds all hollow spaces and crevices, as well as the back of the wall, should be filled with a good soil, so that each and every stone is firmly bedded. The best soil for this purpose is composed of a mixture of turfy loam, peat and well-rotted cow or horse manure. To prevent the soil being washed out of the crevices and joints, the stones must be laid in such a way that the vertical joints of consecutive layers are not immediately above each other — they should be staggered and the spaces kept as narrow as possible. When possible, plants should be set in place as the construction work is done, as this is easier than planting after the erection of the wall has been completed. In the event that it is not possible to plant during the process of building, the best thing to do later is to mix suitable seeds with a little soil and sufficient water to make it moist, and to press this well into the crevices between the stones. The seeds will soon germinate, and establish themselves more quickly than small plants set into the crevices after the dry wall has been completed.

PLANTS FOR THE ROCK GARDEN

Although it is possible, by choosing suitable plants, to extend the flowering period from February to October, the peak period of Alpine flowers is from April to June. Therefore, unless some late-flowering plants are included, the rockery may lack colour during late summer and autumn. For this reason, if no other, it is advisable to consult a specialist grower's catalogue, which will usually give details of a plant's mode of growth, its flowering period and method of cultivation.

The following lists only a few of the many Alpine plants that are available from a specialist nurseryman.

Acaena are long-lived, rapidly-spreading carpeting plants. *A. microphylla* has bronze-purple leaves and red flower bracts. *A. novaezealandiae* has coppery leaves and brownish flower heads. Both flower from June to September.

Achillea does best in a sunny position. *A. agrentea* has silvery foliage, with heads of white flowers between May and June.

Alyssum like a well-drained and sunny position; grow well in poor, dry soil. *A. saxatile* is a greyish, spreading plant with masses of bright yellow flowers during April-May.

Arenaria are dwarf, creeping plants. Most need dividing and replanting every April.

Aster. A number of the dwarf perennial kinds are useful inclusions in the rock garden. They like a sunny position and a soil which is not too dry.

Aubrieta. Available in a number of varieties. They prefer well-drained soil, with some lime, and a sunny position.

Campanula contains numerous varieties, and is valuable for extending the flowering period in the rock garden. Requires a sunny position, and prefers a well drained soil. Some are slow growing, while others spread rapidly.

Cheiranthus, the well-known wallflower, are ideal for the wall garden and will grow in the poorest soil, but require plenty of sun. There are a number of varieties.

Cotyledon. A long-lived plant which is suitable for sun or shade. *C.*

Fig. 7.2   Plants for the Rockery
Top left: *Acaena microphylla*
Top right: *Geranium*
Bottom left: *Omphalodes cappadocica*
Bottom right: *Gentiana acaulis*

simplicifolia has leathery green rosettes. During June-August it bears beady yellow flowers from arching sprays.

Dianthus is ideal for a well-drained, sunny position and numbers a choice of varieties. Whilst most are long-lived, *D. deltoides* has only a shortish life.

Erodium are generally long-lived if planted in a sunny position. *E. chrysanthum* has grey, ferny foliage and soft yellow flowers. *E. guttatum* is a low, grey-leaved plant with red-marked, pale pink flowers.

Gentiana comprise three groups: spring-flowering, summer-flowering and autumn-flowering. They are inclined to be particular in their demands, and can be a complete failure if they rebel against the soil or situation. Spring-flowering kinds require a sunny aspect and will grow in soils containing lime. Summer-flowering types are possibly the easiest to grow, with or without lime in the soil. However, they do need plenty of sunshine. The autumn-flowering gentians require semi-shade and, with few exceptions, will not thrive in soils which contain lime. These latter plants grow with grassy-stems, bearing trumpets in varying shades of blue.

Geranium, often known as **cranesbill,** is available in a number of varieties. Given a sunny position, these are reliable, long-lived plants which do well in the rockery.

Gypsophila, given a sunny position, are long-lived and make good plants for the wall garden. *G. fratensis* trails exstensively from a central rootstock and bears a good show of clear pink flowers.

Helianthemum, **the rock rose,** are popular, long-lived plants. They require a sunny position, and carry flowers, both double and single, from 1/2-1 inch (13-26 mm) in diameter, depending upon the variety. There are many named varieties in white, pink, yellow, red and orange. The foliage varies from ash-grey to light and dark green. Some grow close to the ground; others are erect and bushy.

Iberis. **The candytuft.** Useful evergreen plants, ideal for walls. Need plenty of drainage and sunlight. A number of long-lived varieties.

Leontopodium, otherwise known as **edelweiss,** is not long-lived.

L. alpinum has silvery tufts and white flowers. Easy to grow in a sunny position on light soil.

Linum. the flax is long-lived, and prefers a well-drained soil in full sunlight. *L. extraxillare* makes strong clumps, with semi-prostrate stems. During May-July it bears light blue flowers.

L. salsoloides nanum has white flowers on trailing stems, which are quite prostrate.

Lychnis is fairly long-lived, and enjoys a well drained, sunny site. *L. flos-jovis* makes hats of silvery-grey, woolly leaves. It bears bright

Fig. 7.3 Plants for the Rockery (cont.)
Top left: *Saxifraga umbrosa*
Top right: *Sedum spectabile*
Bottom left: *Erica carnea*
Bottom right: *Erica terminalis*

pink flowers during May-July. This plant is commonly known as the **campion.**

Omphalodes. Navelworts are good ground cover plants for a semi-shaded position; long-lived. *O. cappadocica* has greyish leaves, the sprays of bright blue flowers appearing April-May.

Oxalis. Some species of shamrock are inclinded to be invasive. They require a sunny situation, but must be kept in check. All are long-lived.

Penstemon likes sun and good drainage. *P. pinifolius* makes neat, small-leaved bushy clumps which, during July to October, bear bright scarlet flowers.

Phlox like a gritty soil and a sunny position. The mat-forming Alpine kinds tend to be long-lived. A good choice of varieties from which to select suitable plants.

Polygonum make useful ground-cover plants, suitable for sun or shade, and form mat-like long-lived growth.

Potentilla. Long-lived, easily grown plants for sunny situations.

P. fragiformis has bright yellow flowers and soft grey leaves.

P. nitida bears pink flowers, and forms silver-leaved hummocks.

Pulsatilla. P. vulgaris — the pasque flower — requires a gritty, well-drained soil which contains lime. It also needs plenty of sunshine. The flowers appear April-May, and are goblet-shaped, with pointed petals. The blooms are shaded from white to mauve, violet-purple and red, with golden anthers. The flowers are followed by ferny leaves and fluffy seed heads.

Saponaria. The soapwort — *S. ocymoides* — is a vigorous trailing plant which becomes a massed sheet of bright pink flowers during May-July.

Saxifraga are known to most gardeners. They are divided into different sections, according to their habit of growth.

Kabshia section: These prefer gritty, but not parched soil in a shaded situation. An open aspect facing north is ideal. The plants in this section are all miniature forms which form tight, rosetted cushions.

Aizoon section: The encrusted *saxifrages* prefer sun and a well-drained soil, but will succeed in ordinary garden soil. They form larger rosettes which are silvery-grey and encrusted.

Porphyrion section: These are prostrate and bear stemless flowers. *S. oppositifolia* forms a low, dark green mat with bright pink flowers.

Mossy section: The plants in this section will grow in partial shade, and prefer a soil which is not too dry. They form bright, evergreen rosetted cushions, and grow fairly rapidly. They flower profusely in spring, and have a fair degree of spread.

Numerous *saxifrages* will be found listed in the catalogues of Alpine specialists, and very many will succeed when planted outdoors.

Sedum. The common stonecrop is so well known that it scarcely needs description. *S. acre, S. dasyphyllum* and *S. album* are weed-like in habit and therefore best avoided. However, there are a number of others which have a more desirable form, some with purplish foliage, some gold, some with white flowers and some with pink or gold.

Sempervivum. There are around 200 kinds of **'houseleek'** in cultivation, and a specialist catalogue should be consulted. They are long-lived, and form evergreen rosettes of limited spread. They will flourish in many situations, including the dry wall, and in poor but well-drained soil (provided the position is sunny) with hardly any attention.

Thymus is a useful, rapidly spreading carpet plant. Most types of thyme require sun and are generally long-lived, with aromatic foliage.

Veronica contains several species, some dwarf and erect, others prostrate and trailing. They require well-drained soil in an open position.

Viola are free-flowering, but short-lived. Most require a sunny position. *V. gracilis* and its hybrids are well known as showy rock plants.

Zauschneria, the **California Fuchsia,** requires a sunny position, and a light soil. Under good conditions they are long-lived, and have a twiggy, bushy mode of growth. During August-October the plants bear scarlet, tubular flowers.

Apart from plants, many dwarf shrubs and confers are admirably suited for cultivation in the rockery and, again, a specialist growers catalogue should be carefully studied.

GENERAL MANAGEMENT

Rock plants, as a general rule, like to remain where they are without disturbance for a number of years; normally it is only necessary to remove weeds and keep the soil surface as open as possible, cut away dead flowers (unless the seed is required) and give an occasional top-dressing.

Top-dressings vary according to the types of rock plant being grown. Some, such as tender Alpines, which are apt to "damp-off" in wet or cold weather, are best protected by a top-dressing of small stone chippings. Where the soil gets washed away from the crowns of the plants, a top-dressing of a sandy, fibrous loam will be beneficial. Lime-loving plants will welcome a top-dressing of crushed lime rubble.

Special care must be taken during the winter, for it is a time when rock plants can be all to easily lost. Cold is not the chief trouble; rain and fog are much more of a problem. That is why a top-dressing of chippings around the plant crowns is useful. It will help to prevent the collection of moisture on this vital part of the more tender plants. In many cases it would be wise to shelter the plants. Sheets of glass. supported by wires, can be erected roof-like above the plants, and this will divert much of the rain away from the protected plants.

THE HEATHER GARDEN

Although not strictly part of the rockery garden, the heathers are mentioned because they can be usefully employed in the design of the overall water garden scheme.

Ericas, or **Heathers,** are grown nowadays much more widely than in previous times. The reason is not hard to find; they are useful in so many ways. Their evergreen foliage can be obtained in a number of varying shades of green, as well as golden-yellow, and they do not spread too much. They are ideal subjects for planting alongside a stream, edging paths, or placing at the front of a border. They are first class as smotherers of annual weeds, and require minimal attention. They do not like being grown beneath deciduous trees, but enjoy a position in full sun.

Heathers will make an attractive feature, especially if they are grown in irregular drifts of one variety, rather than having single specimens of many varieties. By carefully selecting the varieties it is possible various heathers can be chosen to ensure flowers throughout the whole year. Growers catalogues will indicate the flowering periods, and this will assist in making the best selection.

VARIETIES

The varieties chosen will be largely governed by the type of soil in which they are to be grown, especially by the presence or absence of lime. All species will flower in soil which is lime-free, and contains plenty of well-decayed humus. However, generous dressings of peat will be of benefit in all situations. Clay soil of a heavy nature is not suitable for the cultivation of the heathers, and they will do poorly if given such a position.

Fortunately there are some heathers, such as the winter flowering varieties of *Erica carnea, E. darleyensis,* and *E. mediterranea,* which will provide a showy display despite the presence of lime, although they will do better if, before planting, generous dressings of leaf-mould, peat and lime-free compost are added to their growing position.

It is possible to obtain heathers which grow to varying heights, and have different spreads of growth. However, they can be kept in bounds by clipping them back after they have flowered — this will cause them no harm.

Space the plants about 18 inches (457 mm) apart, in drifts of 3 to 5 plants. This will eventually provide an excellent display.

CONIFERS

Conifers can be planted to add interest, scale and colour in the water garden and rockery scheme, for most are evergreens and come in all shapes and sizes, from dwarf to the very tall. the choice of tree is enormous, and care should be taken in the selection to ensure that only specimens suitable to the chosen position are purchased. Companies which specialise in growing conifers normally issue a catalogue with guidance notes which will include the height to which the tree will eventually grow. However, whenever possible try to visit the nursery, and, after explaining what is required, obtain the expert's advice — for a pretty little tree could become a monster with the passage of time.

Most conifers are fairly tolerant of the soil conditions in which they are to grow. Nevertheless, they will respond better if the ground has been well-dug and enriched with fertiliser before they are planted into position. After planting, with their roots well-spread, they should be watered — under no circumstances should the roots be allowed to dry out before the tree has become firmly established. If the site is exposed to cold winds, the tree should be given some protection to shield it. Without protection it may suffer the effects of wind-burn where the wind strikes it, resulting in browning of the foliage and a lop-sided appearance from which it may not recover.

These trees can be safely grown in close proximity to the water, for, being evergreen, they will shed very little in the way of leaves or other harmful matter, to be deposited in the pool. This welcome fact allows the prostrate varieties to be planted close to the water's edge, where they can be used to pleasing effect, giving natural shade and softening the hard boundary between land and water.

The conifer is, however, most useful on and around a rockery, where the dense foliage will retard the growth of weeds through lack of sufficient light. On the other hand, many conifers will grow quite happily in a shady position and may therefore be grown on the side of the rockery which receives only minimal sunlight.

The tall, slender type of conifer can be used as a focal point, acting either as a feature or to draw the eye away from some less attractive subject. When planted close together, the upright dwarf trees will make an excellent contrast with their prostrate neighbours, but some thought should be given, beforehand, as to the ultimate height, size and spread which each may reach.

Planted either singly, or in tight little groups, the taller-growing types will add an attractive feature to the heather garden, where the colours of the heather and form of the conifers can provide an all-year interest to the scene.

As with the heathers, so the conifers can be obtained in a variety of colours. Bluish, grey or greens ranging from light to dark shades. Some forms have yellow or gold tinged foliage. These colour variations can be utilized to provide further contrasts by having one form or another growing near to another. They should, however, be chosen with discretion, as in time they may become too large. The smaller the garden, the more care is needed to choose the slow-growing kinds, even if it does take several years before it stands out as a feature.

Conifers can, of course, also be used for hedging or to form screens. If used for either of these purposes they should be trimmed in May or June to keep the height and spread within reasonable bounds and encourage the density of foliage. But again be absolutely certain that the garden is of sufficient size to support this type of hedge when it is full-grown.

Chapter 8

LAWN MAKING

The neat, green lawn is possibly the most typical feature of an English garden, and the restful green colouring is certainly the best, and most natural setting for the water garden. Only the care devoted to the preparation and maintenance by the gardener will give it that much admired, smooth, even surface and the springy buoyancy and trim neatness that is the hall-mark of the perfect lawn.

LEVELLING THE SITE

Levelling can entail hard work, so if a lawn is already made, unless it is very uneven, the amateur gardner will be well advised to leave it as it is, merely improving the surface gradually by top-dressing and regular rolling.

Levelling may be either to make the plot level in all directions like a table top, or to make is similar to a tilted table. The amount of work involved will depend greatly upon the untouched lie of the land — the nearer it is to the required level, the easier the work will be. However, before attempting to alter the level, the first step will be to remove any surface growth, together with all roots and weeds. The fertile top-soil should also be removed and placed out of the way.

The following aids will be found useful: A number of pegs which have had the top 4 inches (102 mm) dipped in white·paint, a spirit-level, a straight-edged length of wood, a garden rake, and a heavy roller.

Begin at the highest point of the plot by hammering a peg into the ground, driving it in to the white-painted portion. This will be the master peg, from which will be obtained the level of the others. Drive in another peg, no greater than the length of the straight-edge from the first to second peg, and hammer down until its top is level with that of the first peg. The level can be ascertained by resting the straight-edge across the two pegs, and then placing the spirit-level on the straight-edge. Hammer the second peg into the ground until the bubble in the spirit-level remains dead true in the centre — the two pegs will then be perfectly level with each other.

Continue to hammer and level a row of pegs right across the plot. By measuring the distance they stand out of the ground, the fall of the land will be discovered. Any necessary adjustments to the level can then be made.

When the required level has been achieved, the ground should be rolled and raked to consolidate the soil. Check the level at intervals, and eliminate any hollows which may appear. Finally, replace the top-soil, raking and firming with the roller, at the same time removing all stones. To create the right surface for sowing grass seed, roll and rake alternately over the whole area. This together with the removal of all large stones, will produce a surface of fine soil, loose and friable, and ready for sowing.

SOWING

Seed sown during late August and early September, though slow to germinate, will make a better turf than spring-sown seed. The warmth of the summer will not have disappeared, and with a reasonable rainfall likely, the germinating seed will produce healthy growth before the cold of winter becomes too severe. Spring-sown seed is often at the mercy of long dry periods, and germination may be somewhat patchy.

When sowing seed by hand, try to choose a windless day, and use at the rate of 2 oz. (56.70 grams) per square yard (0.84 square metres), in order to get a thick carpet of close turf. The seed can be more evenly distributed if it is well mixed with double its quantity of fine, dry soil.

Divide the plot off into strips of equal size, and divide the seed too, to allow the correct share for each. This will help to ensure even distrubution. It is often wise to sow in two directions, half the seed across the plot, and then the other sown in lengthwise strips. Spread a little lawn fertilizer, lightly rake both ways to cover the seed, and finish by lightly rolling.

Do not attempt to cut the grass until it has reached a height of about 2 inches (51 mm), then use a very sharp mowing machine set high so as to just skim off the tops. Any weeds which appear should be pulled out by hand.

LAYING TURF

Turf is generally supplied in strips, cut 3 ft. (915 mm) by 1 ft (305 mm). They should be laid while still fresh and green, but before this

Fig. 8.1   A Lawn adds to the Charm of a Garden

is done they should be carefully gone over, and all weeds pulled out. It is obviously much easier to remove weeds at this stage, rather than after the turves have been laid.

When laying the turves, pack them closely together, preferably in a pattern similar to that employed by bricklayers in laying bricks. When the turves have been laid they will need to be well watered, and then beaten down with a turf mallet, or with the back of a spade.

If during the first few weeks the weather is dry, it will be necessary to water frequently to prevent the turves drying out. Also, after mowing, the lawn should be rolled.

Ideally, turf should be laid during fine weather, in spring or autumn. Autumn is the better time, and autumn-laid turves will provide a useable lawn by the following summer.

GENERAL CARE

The best time to water the lawn is early in the evening, after the heat of the day has passed. If water is given in the day-time the hot sun and air will dry the moisture up so quickly that the grass will derive little benefit from it. It is a wise rule not to water an established lawn unless absolutely necessary. If watering is commenced it will have to be continued at least once a week during the remainder of the dry spell. Instead of this, run the mower over the lawn frequently, without using the grass-box, and leave the grass lying where it falls, so that it may form a protection for the lawn. There are exceptions to this rule concerning watering. In the case of a young lawn, the seedling grass requires watering every day until it has become firmly established. The same applies to a newly-laid turf lawn. Unless this is kept watered until it has become well set, and the grass well-rooted, it will dry out, and wear patchily.

ROLLING

It is advisable to roll lawns periodically during both the summer and winter, altering the direction of the rolls from time to time. Rolling should be done when the weather is fine, but not too dry or frosty. It is only intended to spread or "tiller" the grass and keep the surface even, not to level the lawn. Never roll the lawn when it is wet and sodden, as this causes a hard crust to form on the surface which impedes drainage and prevents air from getting to the roots of the grass.

CUTTING

Try not to let the grass grow longer than 2 inches (51 mm), otherwise it will start to deteriorate and will take some time to get back into condition. Cut the lawn at least twice every week during the growing season, and occasionally during the winter, choosing a fine day for doing so. Grass continues to grow during the cold months and unless it is cut now and then will become ragged and untidy.

FERTILISATION

At least once a year treat the lawn with a good fertilizer, and top dress occasionally with well-decayed manure, leaves, turf or other vegetable matter. Soil from hotbeds, leafmould, breeze, sand, etc., may also be used. The use of combined fertilizer and week-killer will help to keep the lawn in good condition. **Take care not to use these compounds in areas which will allow them to come into contact with the water features.** Stubborn, deep-rooted weeds should be removed by hand. Wage constant war against weeds, otherwise they will eventually ruin the lawn.

MOSS

Moss is an indication that all is not as it should be, and the cause should be remedied. They problem may be due to compaction of the turf and/or waterlogging. To eradicate the moss, apply a mercurised moss control during the early spring. However, **care must be taken to ensure that none can possibly enter the water.** The application of this control should keep the lawn free of moss for the next twelve months. If the problem is due to the ground being waterlogged, the drainage should be improved to effect a cure. Aeration of the grass roots should be attended to by plunging the tines of a garden fork at close intervals over the lawn — this task can be eased by employing one of the tools specially manufactured for this purpose which make use of hollow tines. It is also beneficial to rake the lawn surface regularly, vigourously raking a number of times in directions at right angles to each other. This will help spread any worm casts, remove moss, dead grass and any other debris, and allow air and water to penetrate the lawn surface.

DRAINAGE

Aeration and scarification are both important — the treatment is necessary to maintain a healthy turf and aid the drainage, so that rain is prevented from remaining on the surface and being absorbed by debris, which would create the ideal conditions for disease. The surface drainage will be aided if a top-dressing of sharp sand and gypsum is spread liberally over the turf after the surface has been spiked or treated with hollow tines, and worked well in. Should this treatment fail to cure the problem, or if the surface holds excessive water in puddles which are very slow to drain away, it will be necessary to put in a system of sub-surface drainage pipes. An alternative is to top-dress each autumn for some years, with breeze, until a cure becomes apparent. This latter method, however, is not as satisfactory as a true drainage system, nor is it so quickly effective. Obviously, this problem can be avoided to a large extent by carefully assessing the land before laying a lawn and, if thought necessary, incorporating drainage at that stage.

THE CHAMOMILE LAWN

Although very much more costly than the more usual lawn of grass, chamomile is an alternative that will resist drought and remain green; it is also fragrant.

Anthemis noblis is the particular chamomile used for lawns. It is also a medicinal herb. A free-branching perennial of spreading habit, it can be established in any ordinary garden soil. The leaves are downy and fragrant, which makes the lawn very pleasant to walk upon. The chamomile lawn can be cut in the same way that grass can be cut; on the whole it is stronger than most lawn grasses and so will stand for more wear and tear. When established it presents a beautiful dark-green sward.

Seed is sown in early April, on ground prepared as for the ordinary lawn. Alternatively, plants can be set approximately 6 inches (152 mm) apart, and by the end of the season they will have covered the area and produced a lovely scented carpet to delight all who step upon it.

Chapter 9

PATHS, PAVING AND OTHER FEATURES

The previous pages have covered the essential aspects of creating a water garden. However, there are some other features which most gardeners will consider necessary or desirable. In this chapter the construction of some of those features will be considered and, of course, foremost amongst these is the path.

PATH CONSTRUCTION

The first essential is to excavate the soil in order to allow a foundation of good drainage material. A six-inch (152 mm) depth of rubble or clinker will be sufficient under normal circumstances, and this should be rolled to consolidate it and make it firm. In some situations it may be desirable to incorporate side drains, or, if the site is particularly difficult, it may be necessary to put in a drainage pipe under the centre of the path.

There are a number of materials which are suitable for the surfacing of paths. These include concrete, stone or precast slabs, crazy paving slabs, and bricks or gravel.

Gravel paths should be made with a slight camber; that is to say, the centre portion should be slightly higher than the sides. The gravel is laid over the foundation and well rolled to create a truly firm surface. A well-made gravel path should remain well-drained in even the wettest weather. However, it is liable to frost damage and may require re-rolling each year to consolidate it.

Concrete paths are also laid with a camber, over a good foundation of drainage material, to a thickness of at least two inches (51 mm).

PAVED PATHS

Paved paths are more picturesque than plain concrete or gravel. Whether the paving is rectangular or crazy is a matter of personal preference. The secret of success in making paths of this kind is to lay the paving dead level. Otherwise the path is made in exactly the same way as the gravel or concrete path, over a layer of rough material.

Ideally, crazy paving should never be laid entirely in cement. Though cement may be used to fill between some of the stones, some soil-filled cracks should be left here and there to be set with carpet plants. A perfectly safe and even path can be made if the slabs have a level surface, and if they are laid accurately. Spread a little fine soil or sand over the rough drainage material, and then bed them into this, using a board as a straight-edge to test the evenness of the surface as the slabs are laid.

Between the cracks of the paving stones (where cement is not employed) a good soil mixed with sand should be rammed, the slabs being made very firm, so that they do not move when trodden on. Tiny plants can be set at the same time as the path is laid, or seeds of suitable plants can be mixed with soil put between the paving. In a very short time such a crazy-paved path will assume a long-established, old-world appearance.

An alternative to the crazy-paved path or the more formal pathway of rectangular paving slabs, is one of bricks laid in an ornamental pattern. The bricks can be used to create various designs, such as herring-bone, or in any other desired fashion the ingenious gardener may decide upon. They may be laid in the same manner as crazy-paving, or bedded into concrete with raked-out joints.

A very happy idea is to set rectangular slabs, a short pace apart, into the grass. This will create an attractive feature, and has the advantage of making a clean pathway usable at all seasons, while the severity of an entirely paved walk is softened by the grass. In order to facilitate cutting the grass, the slabs should be very slightly sunken so that the cutting blades cannot be damaged.

The essential thing with all paths is to arrange good drainage, and ensure that the centre is raised slightly higher than the sides to prevent water collecting on the path where it is trodden.

PAVING

A paved area on a patio, or surrounding a pool, has the main advantage of drying quickly, allowing you to relax on a firm, dry surface, even though it may have been raining hard some days previously. It must, however, be well constructed, with the safety factor kept very much in mind, especially if the area is to be used for outdoor meals and recreation to which friends and relatives will be invited.

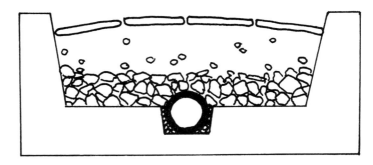

Rubble and drainage-pipes ensure an easy escape for surface water

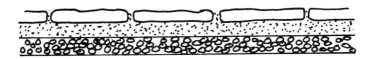

Paving stones are laid on a bed of sand, over a well-drained sub-strata

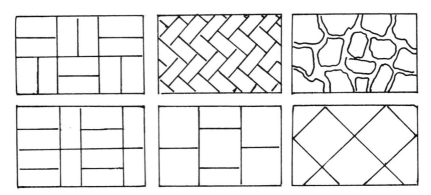

Paving can be laid in various patterns, from different materials such as slabs, crazy paving and hard bricks

Fig. 9.1 Paths and Paving

TYPES OF PAVING

Extremely decorative paved areas can be made by the use of the various materials which are available to add charm to the small, walled garden. To a certain degree the choice of material will depend upon the anticipated wear the surface is to take, and whether it will harmonize with the surroundings. Care must be taken to avoid the combination of too many varied materials in the design, otherwise the final result might look like a jig-saw puzzle. Rectangular paving interspersed with cobble-stones, for instance, will serve to give interest to what might otherwise be a dull, plain surface.

Stone paving in either natural or artificial form is possibly the most popular type of paving material, and one of the easiest to lay. Natural stone slabs tend to be expensive, but if the cost can be met, an area paved with good quality material such as York sandstone will have a character quite distinct from one paved with artificial slabs. A compromise between plain concrete and natural stone type paving would be to use artificial stone. This man-made, imitation paving is made from a mixture of crushed natural stone and cement. Various pigments or coloured aggregate are often added to give a variety of different colours and textures, and they are usually available in various shapes.

Bricks can be used to create interesting patterns, but, due to their small size, are tedious to lay over a large area. Although bricks are available in a variety of colours, allowing a choice that will blend in with any other nearby brickwork, only dense, hard-burnt bricks should be used. Soft bricks will not wear well and will start to break up after heavy frosts. Often suitable bricks can be obtained from demolished buildings; these will create an immediate weathered aspect to the paved area.

Always ensure that the thickness of the paved area, including the foundations, is adequate to take the weight of people and garden furniture. Under normal circumstances a 2 inch (51 mm) thickness will be sufficient for general use as a recreation area. Most paved areas should be given a slight fall of, say, 2 inches in 10 feet (50 mm in 3 m) to enable all surface water to drain away. An important point, where a paved area abuts against the wall of a building, is to ensure that it does not come above the damp-proof course. To avoid any serious future problems in the structure of the building, such as rising damp, keep the paving at least 6 inches (150 mm) below the damp-proof course, or leave a widish gap between the paving and the masonry, although this is not the best method.

LAYING THE PAVING

The method used to lay the paving will, to some extent, depend upon the material being used. Generally speaking, there are two basic methods: one is to bed the paving on a layer of sand; the other is to lay it in mortar upon a concrete base.

There are some disadvantages to the first method — the surface may soon become uneven, and weeds can push their way through the gaps in the paving. It is nevertheless a quick and easy method of laying the paving, and allows rearrangement at a later date if desired. Additional strength can be given by mixing cement with the sand in the proportion of one part of cement to five parts of sand. Lay the "mix" dry, and the underlying dampness will, in a short time, cause the cement to harden somewhat and bind the sand.

Laying the paving on mortar is stronger and more permanent — this should be remembered if there is any possibility that it may have to be altered at a later date. A 2 inch (51 mm) thick concrete base should first be laid over a bed of compacted hardcore, and levelled with the required amount of fall. The paving is then bedded with mortar, on top of the hardened concrete. This should be done with care, to avoid any mortar overflowing onto the paving. Finally, the joints are carefully pointed, or a very sloppy mix can be poured into the gaps. The mortar joints should be smoothed before they set firm, and any overflow removed with a soft brush, to leave a neat finish.

Incorporating a decorative cobble-stone panel or border is quite straightforward. Soak the stones for about 15 minutes in water, before bedding them into mortar. Use a mix of one part cement to two of sand, to bind the stones strongly in place.

PERGOLAS

The use of a **pergola** in the garden will serve not only to provide a shaded area but, in many cases, a degree of privacy. The structure is enhanced by being clothed in climbing plants such as roses, clematis, wistarias and, perhaps, vines, and can be used to give seclusion to a patio which is overlooked by neighbouring windows.

CONSTRUCTION

The material used in the construction depends partly on the use to which the pergola is to be put, and partly on the material used for any other architectural features, even for the house. Stone piers with sub-

Fig. 9.2 Pergola Styles
In the right setting, pergolas can be attractive features

stantial oak runners will give a solid, dignified appearance to a **pagoda** set in a large garden. In other situations, where something less imposing would be more suitable, peeled or unpeeled pine poles will create an attractive rustic effect. In the modern housing-estate garden, squared, hard timber may be more in keeping with the architecture of the house or bungalow.

The upright posts should be treated with preservative before being sunk to a depth of 24 inches (610 mm) into the ground. They should stand above ground to a height of around 8 feet (2.44 m). The top cross rails must be very firmly attached to the upright posts to prevent one falling and possibly causing an accident.

All pergolas should be well furnished with climbing plants, which can be grown either in a long continuous bed, or in small square or circular beds that surround the feet of the posts.

Wooden pergolas should be constructed of very durable timber — climbing plants take some time to become established and, if soft wood is used, the pergola may break just as the plants reach their full beauty.

FENCES AND SCREENS

In general, the ownership of a fence can be ascertained by inspection of the deeds of the property. Usually it is safe to assume that if the posts and rails face onto the garden, then the fence belongs to that garden. If, on the other hand, the posts and rails face onto an adjoining garden, the fence will belong to that owner.

Modern types of fencing of the prefabricated type allow very quick, easy erection and, if plastic or plastic coated, will require very little maintenance. Also, the different types of fencing panels are both decorative and reasonably long-lasting. Other sorts of fencing are all easily made/or erected by the average person, with a little care and thought.

No matter what kind of fence is chosen, they must all be adequately supported to withstand the pressure of high winds. Timber posts with a diameter of about 4 inches (102 mm) will support most fences. However, in very exposed positions concrete posts would be a better proposition. Pack the posts firmly in their holes with rubble, or by setting in concrete. Wooden posts should be soaked for 24 hours in a wood preservative before use, to avoid rotting — only the section going into the ground requires this treatment.

Fig. 9.3 Pergola with Brick Piers and Oak Posts

SCREENS

The purpose of a screen, as its name implies, is to hide an ugly view of some part of the garden so that it does not detract from the beauty of the garden. The screen may be in the form of a hedge, fence, pergola or wall, and should harmonize with the rest of the garden. If there is any preference it should be for a type that is attractive to look at, and will gain beauty with age. It should also be long-lasting. If used to hide buildings or compost heaps, the screen can be arranged in such a way that it overlaps, but leaves a way between the two sections, to allow access behind them.

The artificial screen may be constructed from a durable wood, or with one of the various decorative open-work walling blocks. The former should have the same attention given to the stability of the uprights posts as was recommended for those of the pergola. Screens built up from courses of mortar-jointed ornamental walling blocks will require a solid foundation of concrete. Depending upon the length and height of the wall, it may be necessary to ensure stability by incorporating pillars at intervals.

The attraction of any screen, no matter how well-made, can be improved by adding the beauty of climbing plants to its face. As the climbers become established they can be trained to provide cover for much of the bareness of the artificial structure, giving it a softer and more natural appearance.

BRIDGES

If it is to be used for other than purely ornamental purposes, a bridge must be well-made, allowing safe passage for those who wish to cross from one side to the other. Possibly the easiest method is to firmly lay two or three railway sleepers tightly side by side, sinking them flush with the surface of the ground. If desired, uprights, carrying side-rails or hand-ropes, can be securely attached with long screws to the sleeper sides.

The handyman will, no doubt, think of other methods of bridge construction, but, in all cases, it must be sturdy enough for its purpose.

STATUARY

An original design is usually very expensive. However, many of the mass-produced pieces of statuary are very pleasing, and compari-

Water Maids

Fish Boy

Water Carrier

Rock Baby

Fig. 9.4   Examples of Statuary

tively cheap. They are available in all shapes and sizes. Some are quite beautiful, others ugly and grotesque; in between are some which are bright and merry. The type which will appeal to one person will not be the choice of another, but when selecting any piece of statuary careful consideration should be given. Consider the site it is to occupy and try to decide on the size and style best suited to that position. Haphazard selection can be fatal, so decide what you are looking for before setting out to make a purchase.

Lead figures weather nicely, taking on a very lovely hue, and do not wear away. Artificial stone ones, however, although they often become coloured, may flake rather badly over a period of time.

The design chosen should give lasting pleasure to those who must live with it, and express a mood suitable to the position in which it is to be placed. Again, a figure should always be placed for some purpose — to provide a focal point in a design which will arrest the eye.

Fig. 9.5   Ornamental Frog

VASES AND TUBS

Vases and tubs provide the means of maintaining a succession of colour on the paved terrace or patio. They are also useful for growing small ornamental trees in similar situations.

Although it is possible to construct suitable containers at home, it is generally much easier to purchase ready-made tubs and vases. These are available in materials ranging from wood and stone to the modern moulded plastics, in varying styles, sizes and designs. Wine casks, cut in half and suitably painted, are ideal for mass-planting or accommodating small trees which require plenty of root space. All tubs and vases should be provided with drainage holes.

Chapter 10

ELECTRICITY IN THE GARDEN

BEAUTIFY YOUR POND

There is little doubt that even the most beautiful of ornamental pools, especially in the formal design, will become much more alive if a fountain plays upon its surface. Furthermore, no natural or informal water garden is truly complete without a waterfall. But, to incorporate either — or perhaps both — the modern water gardener must rely upon electricity to run the necessary pumps. There is also a growing trend to install lighting in some areas of the water garden. Certainly there is maximum visual effect when the cascade or a waterfall or fountain spray is lit at night. Even more breathtaking is the visual impact of a pool which has underwater lighting.

WORK FOR THE EXPERT

Before adding any of these facilities, however, consider whether you know enough about electricity in the garden for the installation of electric cables and fittings, and their connection to the main electric supply, it is most certainly the province of only those who are fully skilled in such things. This is certainly true when such work is to be carried into the garden, and it is best left to the expert electrician.

Once electricity is taken beyond the interior of the house you will be operating in an exceedingly dangerous area, and in the garden the potentially dangerous electricity can become lethal. This danger is greatly increased when electricity and water are in close proximity, unless it is installed with a proper regard to ensuring absolute safety. Unless there is a proper earth connection to provide some protection, you could sustain a dangerously violent shock capable of killing you. This does not mean that electricity should not be used outside. It does mean, however, that the correct type and quality of cable for exterior use is employed, and only those fittings designed and approved by law, for *outside use* should be fitted. Sockets, switches and the like should all be adequately screened and protected from the effects of the weather — a most necessary precaution — and all connections must be properly and safely made. **Under no circumstances should a fitting intended for indoor use be installed outside.**

The laws relating to outdoor wiring, and the use of electricity, can differ from country to country, but generally most have one thing in common — a regard for safety, to prevent mains power from running to earth through the body. Proper insulation and earthing and/or other safety measures are stipulated for each situation in which electricity is likely to be employed.

U.K. REGULATIONS

In Britain there are strict regulations in respect of any permanent outdoor wiring installation. These insist that all switches, sockets and lighting fittings must be thoroughly weatherproof. Only pvc-insulated and sheathed cables may be used, and they must be set in a high strength plastic or galvanised steel conduit to protect them from accidental damage. The conduits containing the cables must be either fixed to a wall, or buried below ground to a depth of not less than 18 inches (457 mm). The regulations forbid the fixing of any cables to a fence — which could be blown down in high winds — but they do allow cables to be run overhead. They should be hung from a strong steel suspension wire, which must not be less than 12 feet (3.65 m) above ground at its lowest point. The regulations also stipulate that all metal fittings must be resistant to corrosion, weatherproof and effectively and securely fixed and earthed. All wiring that runs into the garden from the house must be considered as a separate installation and be provided with its own fuse unit and main switch. However, wiring to any lighting fittings or socket outlets attached to the outside walls of a house can be considered part of the existing interior electrical installation.

These rules are not as daunting as they may sound, and are designed with only one aim — safety and the protection of life. There is, after all, little point in designing a beautiful water garden if, each time the electricity is switched on, life is put at risk.

CONTROLLING

Ideally, it should be possible to control the operation of the pumps and outdoor lighting from a switch inside the house, thus avoiding the necessity of having to go outside during cold or inclement weather. If desired, the features could be controlled automatically, with an over-ride switch, so that they switch on and off at pre-arranged times. There are two ways of arranging this automatic control.

TIME SWITCHES

Firstly, a time switch can be wired into the controlling circuit. This will switch the power on and off at the same times every day. It may be necessary to alter the setting control in order to allow any difference in the hours of darkness when the unit controls a lighting system, although there is a type, which is more expensive, that has what is known as a "solar dial" and makes its own compensation for the varying hours of daylight. It is even possible to incorporate a system controlled by a photocell. A typical photocell lighting control consists of a main control box which is installed inside the house, whilst the photocell itself, which is a weatherproof unit, is mounted outside where it can read the natural light but not be affected by the lights which it controls.

Both the time switch and the photocell methods of control will automatically switch the units which they control on or off at the set times. This sort of control is probably more applicable to light units than pumps, where it can be arranged for them to operate during the hours of darkness. On the other hand, a time switch could be set to operate a pump during the daytime, switching it off at night in the event that the sound of running water was not welcome after dark.

Modern aquatic equipment is becoming ever more sophisticated and, whilst much of it operates directly from the mains supply, an increasing number of items are being manufactured which operate on a reduced voltage via a transformer.

Obviously, the transformer will need a mains electricity supply, and this is most conveniently provided by constructing a weatherproof box to contain the mains power socket outlet, fixing it firmly to an outside wall of the house. The box should be large enough to comfortably house the transformer, and be very stoutly constructed with solid back, sides and door that can be securely locked to prevent unauthorized interference with the contents. When completed, the box should be primed, undercoated and given two or three coats of good quality exterior-type paint to preserve it and keep the weather out. Drill or cut holes to allow the mains cable to enter and the cable from the transformer to pass out without the need to open the box door.

Fasten the box to the wall, at a height which puts it safely out of harm's way, and lead the mains supply in through the back, using a 2.5 mm two-core and earth pvc insulated and sheathed cable. Connect the mains cable to a metal-clad switched 13 amp socket outlet installed inside the box; ordinary moulded plastic sockets are not permitted by British regulations. Once the outlet is connected, the box will provide a safe control point for the connection of exterior lights, pumps or any other equipment — of reduced voltage — that may be needed in the garden.

WATER PUMPS

Since the advent of the electric water pump it is no longer necessary to install plumbing to carry mains water to the pool for the operation of fountains or waterfalls. These tasks are efficiently arranged by means of the pumps, and the water is circulated rather than being wasted — thus the mains water is only needed for topping-up purposes.

Generally, water pumps for pools fall into two distinct categories: the **surface-type** and the **submersible.** Within these two categories there is a wide range in type, power of output, and price, for the different models available.

The **submersible pump** is extremely easy to install. It is only necessary to place it in position in the water and connect it to the electricity supply. A length of flexible plastic pipe is connected to the pump, and the other end to the fountain head or waterfall. Care should be taken when choosing the pump that one of adequate power is purchased. If it will be required to operate continuously, be sure to select one with that capability, for not all pumps are intended for long periods of non-stop running. Consider the amount of work it will be required to perform and the volume of water it should turn over within a given time, then select accordingly.

The **surface-type pump** is more expensive than the sumbersible type, and is usually used for very powerful work; the submersible are mostly less powerful. It has to be installed outside the pool in a specially constructed housing or chamber as close to the water as possible, and below water level. Installation of this type of pump is quite straight-forward, except that it is a little more time-consuming and complicated. The surface pump draws water from the the pool by means of a flexible plastic pipe and discharges it through another pipe to the fountain or waterfall. Some models are powerful enough to operate several fountains or waterfalls at the same time, or create a waterfall with a high cascade of water.

Fig. 10.1   The Stuart "Water Nymph" Submersible Pump

A low, 24 volts AC pump. It has a plastic body, and a removable strainer for easy cleaning. Operating from a transformer it consumes 65 watts and has a maximum flow rate of 350 gallons per hour.

Fig. 10.2   The Stuart "SSI" Submersible Pump

Operating from AC mains, this pump has a flow rate of 250 gallons per hour and has a protective thermal overload. Suitable for a small pool, it can be used to supply a fountain or waterfall

THE WATERPROOF CHAMBER

These pumps should be housed in a waterproof chamber which can be constructed from waterproof concrete, below which is a well-drained sump. The base of the container should be provided with one or more holes to allow any accumulation of water to escape into the sump. Holes should also be allowed for in the walls, so that the electricity cable and water-pipes can be taken through. The lid should be a good fit and designed to prevent water penetration, making the container waterproof.

Make the container large enough to allow easy installation of the pump and connection of the pipes without undue difficulty — nothing is more annoying than receiving scraped knuckles through lack of working space.

If, for any reason, the pump is not below the water level, a foot-valve should be fitted to the inlet pipe to prevent the pump emptying itself when it is switched off. If, however, the pump is positioned lower than the pool water level a foot-valve will not be necessary. It is also a wise precaution to fit a stop-cock to the suction pipe, so that the flow of water from the pond can be halted when the pump is switched off or removed for servicing. If this is not done the pool water is sure to syphon along the suction pipe and flood the pump container.

Once the required housing has been constructed and the pump installed in position and connected to the inflow and outflow pipes, it only requires that a check be made to discover whether the pump needs priming — some do, others do not — before connecting to the electricity supply and switching on.

The use of these electric water pumps has greatly simplified the movement of water, and has brought with it an added bonus; no longer is it necessary to syphon or bale water when emptying a pool. If a length of hosepipe is connected to the pump outlet, and led to a suitable drainage point, it is only necessary to switch on and let the pump empty the pool.

ILLUMINATION

For those who wish to add after-dark illumination to the water garden, special lighting units are available. Although they can be used in the informal setting to some effect they are, perhaps, more suited to the formal design. The use of these lights will add another dimension to the patio or pool when they are switched on after dusk has fallen,

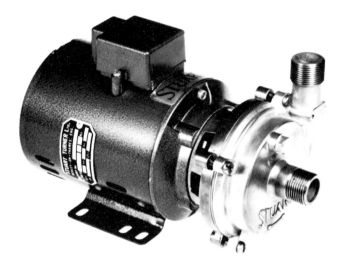

Fig. 10.3   The Stuart "Type 903" Centrifugal Pump

Designed for continuous use, this type of pump is suitable for larger pools where a high water flow is required. It must be housed in a weatherproof external compartment, this particular model having a waterflow of around 1,250 gallons per hour

and this is probably the ideal situation in which to employ these units.

If the feature to be illuminated is near the house it may be possible to use wall-mounted lights. It is a good idea when lighting such places to install adjustable lights that can be aimed at a particular spot. Relatively simple and inexpensive miniature floodlights can be obtained which use PAR (parabolic aluminised reflector) lamps of 100 or 150-watt rating. They consist of a cylindrical metal housing mounted on a ball joint and containing a screw-type lampholder. At one end of the cylinder there is a rubber seal against which the neck of the lamp presses when it is screwed into position, making a weatherproof and watertight seal which is electrically safe. The cable passes out of the other end of the cylinder and has a shielded, weatherproof cable seal.

PAR lamps are very robust and incorporate their own reflector in the form of a bright aluminium coating on the rear surface of the lamp. They are available in a variety of colours, which allows some unusual effects to be obtained.

PORTABLE LAMPS

Features which are some distance from the house can be lit by means of portable lamps. Although mains operated units are available, it is safer to purchase a low-voltage, portable lighting system, which operates through a transformer and is stepped-down to around 12-volts. Complete systems are available comprising transformer, lamps and fixing spikes.

SUBMERSIBLE LAMPS

Special submersible types are made for installing under water, having various coloured sealed-beam lamps in non-corrosive lampholders, which can be either floated upon the water-surface or fastened underwater.

There are also units which operate in conjuction with a fountain. These illuminate the patterns of spray from the fountain jets, and, by means of the appropriate kit, can be arranged to change colours at intervals to give to the night-time scene an unusual and novel attraction.

These low-voltage units are all completely safe and, being isolated from the mains supply, present no electricity hazards. As a result of their high safety factor they are legally accepted in virtually all countries.

POOL HEATERS

Miniature floating electric heaters are available for winter use in the pool. The sole object of using these heaters is to keep open and free of ice, a section of the pool water surface, thus enabling any noxious gases to escape. They are not intended to, nor should they, warm the water to such a degree that the fish and plants become prematurely and unseasonably active. It is only necessary to use a pool heater when freezing conditions threaten.

Chapter 11

MAINTENANCE

ATTENTION IS ESSENTIAL

It is probably true to say that in nature there is no such thing as a truly permanent pool, for having made the pool Dame Nature then conspires to eradicate her work. Leaves are blown into the water, where they decompose; submerged and marginal plants die and rot, and wind-blown dust and other matter finds its way into the pool. In their various ways each eventually become silt on the bottom of the pool. Dying vegetation around the margin of the pool falls and becomes compost, which allows the poolside plants to advance little by little further into the pool. In so-doing the banks encroach further into the water and the water surface area is reduced. Behind the steadily-encroaching marginal plants the ground becomes ever more firm, to be colonized by various forms of terrestrial plant-life.

The reduction of the water surface, combined with the ever-decreasing depth of the pool, leads to a faster and faster rate of evaporation of the remaining water. Eventually the combination of thickening bottom silt and encroaching pool-side banks and vegetation, coupled with the rapid evaporation rate, will lead to the elimination of the pool. The most that may remain to show that a pool once existed may be nothing more than a damp hollow. It may take a great many years, but eventually the pool will disappear. Only very large lakes or areas scoured by a strong through-current of water may manage to survive, but these are not pools in the accepted sense of a small, enclosed body of water.

Despite the claims made by some, there is no such thing as a "balanced pool" in the context of the ornamental pool of average proportions. It pre-supposes a self-sufficiency; an inter-dependent self-supporting system that requires no outside assistance. This, however, cannot be attained, nor would it be desirable in the restricted world of the average ornamental pool. Neglect to feed the fish and they will suffer, for, despite a common belief, there is little likelihood that there will be enough natural food to support a number of fishes. Failure to remove rotting debris and bottom silt will sooner or later result in pollution, with consequential loss of fish.

VITAL CONTROL

In nature each form of life fights for dominance, in one way or another. Creature preys upon creature, each intent upon its own survival. "Eat or be eaten — kill or be killed" is the law of the wild, and so an useasy balance is arrived at. However, this is not the sort of ruthless balance that is wanted in the ornamental pool. Therefore it is essential that we exercise control over the pool to ensure the well-being of the fish and maintain the pool's appearance.

Realising that the ornamental pool cannot be left to take care of itself, the wise water-gardener will develop a method of routine maintenance. Daily inspections will be made to ensure that all is well — fish do die and, occasionally, some other creature may fall into the water and drown. The routine periodic pruning of plants takes less time than is normally devoted to the annual pruning of ornamental shrubs, and cleaning the pool is less laborious than digging a vegetable plot. Such routine maintenance is essential to the continued success of the pool, and should not be neglected.

ANNUAL CLEANING

The annual cleaning can be undertaken during either spring or autumn. In fact, there is no reason why it should not be carried out twice yearly, but if attention can only be given to this task once yearly, then it should be during the autumn. It is surprising the amount of detritus that can accumulate at the bottom of a pool during a period of six months. If the major overhaul is made during the spring, the autumn attention will only require that the pool is drained, all silt and other debris removed, and the pool refilled with fresh water. This will provide clean conditions and reduce the possibility of any noxious gases building up when the pool is frozen over, thus improving the fishes capability to cope with the colder months of the year.

EQUIPMENT AND APPROACH

Equipment required will be a long-handled net a container for the fish, a stiff scrubbing brush and some utensil with which to bale out the silt. The rules to follow are:

1. **Commence by lowering the water to a level that will ease the task of catching the fish, which should be netted and carefully placed into containers of clean water.** Make sure that the water in the containers is at the same temperature as that in the pool, and also move them out of harm's way — it is only too

easy to knock over a bucket of fish in a moment of forgetfulness.

2. When the fish have been safely caught and placed well away from the working area, the plant containers (if any) should be lifted from the pool. Gently hose them down with a jet of water to remove as much blanket-weed and sediment as possible. Remove dead leaves and stems and pick off any strands or mats of algae, to leave the plants and containers as clean as possible. Cover them with wet newspaper, to prevent them drying, and place them in a cool, shady spot that is sheltered from any wind. The remaining water should then be removed to reveal the liquid sludge of bottom silt.

3. Take care when baling out the silt and keep a watchful eye open for any fish that may have buried itself in the sediment. If possible strain the muck through a small mesh sieve to be sure that no fish is accidently lost. The dark, strong-smelling sludge can be disposed of on the garden, where it will help to enrich the soil. Although potentially harmful in the pool, the silt will be beneficial to the terrestrial plants, and the strong smell with quickly disappear when exposed to the air.

4. Repeatedly scrub and hose down the pool interior to get rid of all sediment and algae, removing the accumulated dirty water between each flushing. If a filter is incorporated, connect the hose and backflush until the water runs clear. It will be necessary to drain the water from the pool as the filter is flushed through.

5. Pick over any plants that are growing directly in the pool with the same care as described for the container grown plants.

6. Partially fill and empty the pool a few times to ensure that as much as possible of the remaining fine sediment is removed. The pool is ready for the final filling when any sediment that may still remain quickly settles and the water is clear, without any trace of cloudiness.

7. The plants in their containers can now be replaced and the pond filled with clean, fresh water. Allow the water to run in at a reasonably slow rate, making sure that it does not disturb the planting medium. If it is a warm, dry day the wet paper should be left over the plants to protect them; the paper can be removed after the water level has risen above the plants.

8. Finally, after the pool has been filled and the hosepipe removed, the container of fish can be carefully floated in the pool until the water temperatures have equalised, after which the fish can be released.

CONTROL OF PLANTS AND THEIR PESTS

Given the right conditions all water-plants, whether submerged or otherwise, will establish themselves and then commence to extend their territory. As always, the strongest will be the most successful and, unless strictly controlled, will overpower their weaker neighbours.

Control the rampant growers by removing any adventurous offshoot or seedling. Take out excessive growth by thinning and prunning; where possible remove the older plants to allow the younger growth to develop. The younger plants will be stronger and more vigourous than the older, which may be near the end of their life.

Where a plant reproduces by means of runners, it is best to sever the young plant as soon as it has rooted by cutting through the runner near the parent stock; this avoids the older plant being weakened unduly, and also encourages it to produce further plantlets.

Tuberous rooted plants should be divided by having the newer growth separated from the older root-stock, making sure that is has roots attached and a growing crown.

At times the quality of the various plants may begin to deteriorate — when that time arrives the plants should be lifted, and the young, vigorous growth selected and replanted in a newly replaced planting medium.

On no account should any insecticides or any other form of chemical be used to control insects found in or around the water garden. They could, and very probably will, have a harmful effect upon the fish. Bordeaux mixture, nicotine sprays and other insecticides should be avoided like the plague, for they can all be lethal. Equally, the application of insecticides anywhere near the water should be avoided because, if they enter the pool, the consequences can be tragic.

INSECT PESTS

Various insects may sometimes attack the leaves of water-lilies and other aquatic plants; fortunately they seldom reach uncontrollable limits.

The **brown china-mark** (*Nymphula*) lays its eggs amongst water-side vegetation during June and July, when it deposits rows of eggs on the underside of water-lily and other leaves. The greenish-yellow caterpillars feed upon the leaves, from which they cut oval-shaped pieces. Weight the leaves below water level so that the fish can easily reach the larvae.

Galerucella grisescens, the orange coloured water-lily beetle, is about the size of a ladybird. Although not a true aquatic beetle, it lays its yellowish eggs on the underside of water-lily leaves. The beetle and its eggs will be eaten by the fish, as will the reddish-black water-lily aphis *(Rhopolosiphom)* which may be controlled by flushing them into the water. Use a strong water jet for a number of days, at intervals, until the problem is cured.

ALGAE

Green water is due to free-floating minute algae, and is not a sign of unhealthy conditions. Algae flourish where there is an excess of light and the water tends to be alkaline. Usually the condition will clear if given sufficient time.

If the pool is well stocked with plants, the water will slowly become acid and the growth of the plants, particularly the water-lilies, will reduce the intensity of the light. The addition of chemicals is not recommended; at best they are generally only a short term remedy.

The clouding of water in the early spring is a natural occurrence in the mature pool, and Nature will clear the water in her own time, in her own way. Changing the water will only aggravate the problem. Therefore it is advisable to allow Nature to arrange her own cure.

The type of algae commonly known as **blanket-weed** can be particularly obnoxious and troublesome, as can the sort which forms masses of hair-like growth. If allowed to go unchecked these pests will quickly choke the water plants and strangle the life out of them. Whenever it appears it should be raked out. Take care when removing this pest that no small fish has become enmeshed in it. On no account be tempted to use any chemical control.

TURBID WATER

If the pool water develops a milky aspect, however slight, it is almost certain that the water is polluted. Net the fish, if they are still alive, and drain the pool. Remove the cause of the pollution, clean and refill with fresh water. Make sure that the condition is not allowed to re-occur.

Pollution can arise from over-feeding, when the uneaten food rots; decomposing vegetation; an over-accumulation of rotting debris, and dead fish if of any size, amongst other things. Careful feeding and regular maintenance will help to avoid this problem.

OXYGEN EXHAUSTION

Fish gasping at the water surface may be evidence of a shortage of oxygen in the water. Although hungry fish may rise to the surface to beg for food when someone approaches the pool, they do not usually remain there. Oxygen-starved fish will be reluctant to leave the water suface and will only do so if frightened, returning almost immediately.

An over-large fish population, decomposition of matter, or an over-abundance of submerged plants — any one, or all, may be the cause of a depleted oxygen content. During a hot, dry spell, the water in a pool which is over-crowded may be depleted of oxygen to a level that is too low to support the fish — Orfe will normally be the first to die under such conditions. Bacteria in decomposing matter require oxygen and can affect the oxygen level to a marked degree. During daylight plants take in carbon dioxide through their leaves and convert it into oxygen, which is released into the water. However, during the hours of darkness this process is reversed. Thus too many plants may lead to an excessive build-up of carbon dioxide and a lowering of the oxygen content in the water. This will result in the fish suffering from lack of oxygen, but the condition will normally right itself with the return of daylight.

The oxygen content is also related to the water temperature — the higher the temperature the lower the content. This is usually only a temporary condition and need cause no alarm.

If it becomes evident that there is a continuing lack of the essential oxygen, steps must be taken to remedy the condition. Relief may be given, as a temporary measure, by giving a partial change of water. This must not be relied upon as a permanent cure — it is not! Seek the cause, whether it be an excess of plants or decomposing matter; check that the seemingly healthy plants are indeed alive and strongly rooted. If, after a general tidying and renewal of the water, the condition returns and the fish hang at the surface, it is obvious that the number of fish will have to be reduced.

OVER-FEEDING

It is a sad fact that many people tend to offer pool fish too much food, much of which is left uneaten. The amount of food required depends upon a number of factors, such as the water temperature, the number of fish, and their size. As a rule-of-thumb guide, the fish should never be given more than they can quickly eat within about ten minutes. No fish will eat more food that it requires at that particular time, and that which is left could become a source of possible pollution.

Only offer food when the fish are active. During the cold winter months most fish become semi-dormant, and no food will be accepted. It is unwise to place food in the pool at this time, even if a warm day should encourage the fish into temporary activity.

ICE AND SNOW

It is seldom that a pool will freeze solid in winter, provided it has a minimum depth of 18 inches (457 mm). Even in the most severe conditions there is usually an unfrozen area of deeper water in which the fish can survive, and the depth of water provided governs the margin of safety.

Ice covering the pool surface will seal in, and prevent the escape of any noxious gases which may form. In order to allow these harmful gases to escape, a hole must be kept open in the ice. Never break the ice, since the blows from a hammer can kill the fish by concussion. A far safer method is to drill one-inch (25mm) holes or melt a hole in the ice. Draw off a few inches of water to create an air space below the sheet of ice. The hole will admit oxygen and allow the gases to escape. check the hole each day to ensure that it remains open.

Even during the winter the plants need light in order to survive and provide oxygen. If snow blankets the frozen water surface it will cut out the light and prevent it reaching the plants. This in turn will prevent the plants performing their essential function and they may even die. Snow must therefore be swept off the ice every day.

It is possible to purchase specially made pool heaters, which are very like aquarium heaters, and are connected to an electricity point. It should be of only sufficient wattage to keep an open hole in the ice during freezing weather when placed just below the surface of the water; it should not be rated so high that it warms the water and prevents the fish hibernating.

DAILY CARE

Leaves and other matter will be blown into the pool during the year; during autumn, in particular, a great many leaves will fall upon the pool surface. Each day they should be skimmed off with a net. Not only do they spoil the appearance of the pool, but some of the leaves may be poisonous and a danger to the fish. If allowed to remain they will rot in a very short time, and an excess of decomposing vegetable matter will give rise to pollution of the water. If allowed to continue, the putrid condition will eventually prove fatal to the fish.

For the same reasons, spent water-lily flowers and yellowing lily leaves should also be removed if possible. The removal of dead flowers will encourage the plant to produce further blossoms and preserve the attractions of the pool.

SNAILS

Snails can become a great nuisance in the ornamental pool and are better excluded; no gardener would knowingly introduce snails into the flower borders — why introduce them into the pool? An excess of snails, especially if they are of the genera *Lymnaea* or *Physa* (the pond snail and bladder snail respectively), will feed freely upon the underwater vegetation and can cause considerable damage to the plants. They will also consume fish spawn.

Once snails gain entry to a pool it is virtually impossible to destroy them completely — certainly the fish will not eat them. Far better than cure is prevention by making sure that no snails or their eggs are accidentally introduced into the pool.

FROGS, TOADS AND NEWTS

These creatures may decide to take up residence in the ornamental pool and, provided they are not too numerous, they may be welcomed, for their numbers are rapidly declining. During the time that they are present they will give an added interest to the pool.

Occasionally a male frog may seize of fish in its nuptial embrace, and this may kill the fish. However, it is not that common and the lively, fast-swimming fish are not often caught in this way. The risk only exists during the frogs' breeding season.

When small, the tadpoles of the frog will be eaten by the larger fish. However, they will have no appetite for the tadpoles of the toad and they will be ignored.

PREDATORS

Fish my be taken from the pool by a number of different predators — animal, bird, reptile and even humans have been known to steal fish. Short of stretching a small-mesh net across the pool, little can be done to prevent their attentions once they have discovered the pool.

Within the water, some beetles are predatory. These are impossible to avoid because most have the ability to fly from pool to pool. Possibly the best known is the **Great Diving Beetle,** *Dytiscus,* which can grow to around one-and-a-half inches (38 mm). It is olive-brown in colour with a yellow margin around the thorax and wing-cases. It is very ferocious, and will attack creatures much larger than itself. It has a large-growing larvae that has sickle-shaped mandibles, and is also carnivorous by nature. The larval stage of the **Dragonfly,** although sluggish, is another vicious predator, which lurks in wait for its victim. The widespread **Water Boatman** also feeds upon living creatures, and has little hesitation in attacking those which are larger than itself.

These, and any other predatory beetles, should be removed when seen, and killed. To ignore them is courting trouble, for many can damage a fish quite considerable, even if they do not kill it.*

IN GENERAL

Devote the same care to maintaining the appearance of the water garden as would be devoted to the upkeep of any other form of garden. Under normal circumstances, the chores of looking after the terrestrial features will occupy far more time than is demanded by the watery areas and, generally, be more arduous.

The thoughtfully planned, well-constructed and properly cared for water garden will prove a lasting attraction, and provide many hours of pleasant, relaxing enjoyment — hours that will make hard work and time seem as nothing, when compared to the beauty of your creation.

*Readers who would like to learn more about the various beetles, pests and diseases, together with all other aspects of fish, plants and coldwater life in general should obtain a copy of one, or both, of the author's books *Fancy Goldfish Culture* or *Cyclopaedia of Coldwater Fish and Pondlife.* Both books are published by Nimrod Book Services, who will be pleased to give further details.

Chapter 12

FISH CARE

PREVENTIVE MEASURES

In most cases, the water garden will have its complement of fish, for without the graceful movement of the fishy population no water garden scene would be truly complete. However, in common with all forms of life they can suffer from various maladies, although most problems will normally only arise if circumstances have in some way brought about a lowered resistance. Much can be done to avoid attacks by disease and pests. Of prime importance is the strict observation of quarantine and the disinfection of all new stock, both fish and plant. It is also necessary that the best living conditions are provided — by ensuring that the water is kept healthy — and that proper attention is given to the feeding of the fish. If the rules of good management are followed it is not difficult to keep the fish in a state of good health. Generally, the majority of fish have a great natural resistance to disease so long as they are not weakened by bad treatment, poor or inadequate food, lack of oxygen, rapid fluctuation of water temperature, or some other adverse condition.

If the pool, plants and fish are perfectly clean and healthy to start with, any parasitic infection can only be introduced from an outside source. Parasites may be introduced by insufficiently quarantined and cleaned fish or plants, or live foods obtained from waters containing fish may be responsible. Always exercise care, and parasites are not likely to become a difficult problem.

BASIC SYMPTOMS OF DISEASE

Even when the most careful attention is given to the well-being of the fish it is a sad fact there will almost certainly be times when disease will raise its ugly head. The symptoms of the different diseases will vary according to their nature, but there are a number of signs that will indicate whether the fish may be suffering from some complaint.

The cotton-woolly appearance of a fungus infection is usually easily recognised. Other diseases of the skin are often indicated by a prolonged and noticeable fading of the colours; there may also be a formation of greyish, slimy excretion covering small or large areas of the body. On dark-coloured fish these signs are fairly easily observed, but they may not be so easily seen on the bodies of those with lighter colours. Some skin infections are evidenced by the appearance of white, brown or blackish spots. Irritation of the skin, by disease or parasite, will very often cause the fish to rub itself against various objects — it may also make wild dashes through the water.

Bacterial diseases are generally characterised by the presence of red spots on the skin. Eye infections often result in either a greyish cataract or an enlargement of the eye.

Many diseases will result in the fish lingering near the water surface, with tightly folded fins. Gill infections cause the fish breathing problems. The suffering fish will open its gill coverings much wider than is normal, and the frequency of breathing will be greatly increased. The soft gill-sheets, beneath the hard gill-covers, will become pale, and may have small inflamed areas. Very pale gills are a sure sign of diseases in a living fish; the gills of a healthy fish will always have a bright-reddish colour.

Internal disorders may cause abnormal swellings or, conversely, result in a thin, hollow-bellied appearance. Constipation can cause the fish to go off its food. Within the body of the fish is an organ known as the swim-bladder. Swim-bladder problems results in the victim having difficulty in maintaining its equilibrium — it may make tumbling movements, or have difficulty rising from the bottom. In other instances it may continuously float, like a cork, to the water surface.

AVOID OVER-CROWDING

In general, it can be said that the smaller the number of fish in a body of water the easier it is to control an outbreak of disease; in a densely populated, overcrowded pool a disease can quickly assume epidemic proportions resulting in the loss of many of the fish. This, in itself, is sufficient reason to avoid the mistake of over-stocking, for Nature has her own way of limiting any species which over-populates its habitat, and disease is one of her prime weapons.

CAREFUL OBSERVATION

It should not be thought from the foregoing that the fish will be plagued by ill-health, for it has already been remarked that, with proper care and attention, most fish have a strong natural resistance to infection by disease. Most problems arise from bad management or some action attributable to the fish-keeper. However, observation and an awareness of the signs indicating clearly that all is not well will enable the owner to recognise a possible problem, and take any necessary action before things get out of hand. Whilst not all diseases of fishes are curable, most of those which may infect the pool fish are. Early recognition and treatment of a disease will in most cases give the fish an excellent chance of recovery, whereas neglect can lead to its death.

TYPES OF DISEASES

Fish diseases may be broadly divided into four groups: **bacterial, fungoid, organic** and **parasitic.** In practice, however, it is not always possible to classify many of them with accuracy, for the dividing line is sometimes very finely drawn. However, in general it can be said that bacterial diseases may be recognised by inflamed areas on the skin; **fungoid diseases** by cottonwool-like growths and **parasitic diseases** by the erratic, wild dashing-about movements of the fish, as it knocks itself against firm objects. Some of the larger parasites, such as *Argulus* and *Lernea,* may be clearly visible, attached to the fish. Loss of activity, colour or appetite, though not infallible signs of disease, are indications that the fish is not in the best of health.

Bacterial diseases are largely the result of polluted water. Therefore, whenever there has been an outbreak of a bacterial disease, the pool should be drained and thoroughly cleaned and care taken to ensure that there is no further recurrence of the conditions that caused the water to become polluted.

The spores of fungus are present in all still waters, and are harmless enough when the fishes are in good health — because they are protected by a mucus covering over the body — but will attack a fish in poor health in which the supply of mucus has become inadequate. Fungoid diseases are, generally, a sign of lowered health and vitality. They also tend to be contagious due to the fact that, if conditions have lowered the resistance of one fish, the other fish may well have similar loss of resistance.

Parasitic diseases are due, obviously, to the activity of parasites, and mostly they can only survive when fish are present. If a fish becomes infested with parasites it is reasonable to assume that all fish in the same water will also be infested. If all fish are removed from the pool for a period of around three weeks, the parasites in the pool will die through lack of a suitable host.

RULES TO OBSERVE

Before considering specific complaints and remedies, the water gardener/fishkeeper should learn to observe the following rules:

1. **Do not rush into treating a suspect fish unless it is obviously afflicted by a definite complaint.** Fish, like humans, have their "off-days" and a listless fish may only be feeling a "little under the weather". However, if it persists, and there is real cause for concern, place the suspect fish into a separate container for observation and, if necessary, treatment.
2. **Always ensure that, when moving a fish to an isolation container** (preferably an aquarium to allow easy all-round observation) **or medicinal bath, the water temperature has been adjusted to that of the water from which the fish has been removed.**
3. **Handle the fish as little as possible.** There is no fear of the disease infecting the handler, because no fish disease can be passed to the human, but, like all sick creatures, the fish should not be disturbed unless absolutely necessary.
4. **If a fish is proved to be suffering from an ailment, keep an eye on other fish which have been in contact with it, in case they have also been infected.**
5. **Medicinal baths should be freshly prepared as required, long term baths being renewed daily.**
6. **Should a fish show signs of distress after being placed in a medicinal bath, remove in immediately, and weaken the solution before replacing it.** A close watch should always be kept when immersing a fish in treatment baths, for individual fish can vary in their level of tolerance.
7. **If the fish fails to respond to treatment after a reasonable time, it is kinder to destroy it without further ado.**
8. **Do not over-dose in the belief that it will bring about a speedier cure** — it could well have the opposite effect and result in the death of the fish.
9. **Always wash the hands, and disinfect nets and other equipment, after being in contact with a sick fish.** Failure to observe this elementary precaution may lead to the accidental infection of the healthy fishes.
10. **Encourage the invalid to eat by offering good nourishing food.** If the fish eats its food it stands a better chance of making a full return to health.
11. **Never, never flush carcasses or diseased fish down the lavatory pan. Nor should a sick fish be released into any natural wild**

water. Both actions are to be deplored, for they could ultimately lead to the infection being passed to our native fishes, possibly with devasting results. **Dead fish should be burned, or buried deep in a compost heap,** to avoid the possibility of any infection gaining entry into healthy waters.

SYMPTOMS

Comparison of the obvious signs of illness exhibited by an afflicted fish against the following list of symptoms will enable a reasonably accurate diagnosis to be made of the most probable cause of the malady. By referring to the indicated complaint in the following pages, it will be possible to find the cause of the problem, together with the treatment. It should hardly need saying that, not only must action be taken to cure the complaint, but steps must also be taken to remedy the original cause of the problem.

White cottonwool-like tufts on body or fins — **Fungus.**
White or greyish film on eyes — Cataract.
Fish knocks against firm objects and has a **transparent, flat, greenish creature,** about the size of a ladybird, attached to it — *Argulus.*
Fish act as above and/or has a **cotton thread-like creature** attached — *Lernea.*
Fish rubs and scratches itself, fins twitch, and sudden wild dashes are made. Breathing rate may be accelerated — **Flukes.**
Scales stand out, bloated body — Dropsy.
White pinhead-sized spots on body and fins — *Ichthyophthiriasis.*
Difficulty in swimming. Fish cannot rise from bottom. Floats to surface like a cork. Turns on back. Floats head down — **Swim-bladder trouble.**
Air-bubbles in fins — Air Embolism.
Blood-streaked veins in tail and other fins. Later the fins fray and rot — **Fin-rot.**
Small worm-like creatures attached to fish — **Leeches.**
Slimy, greyish-white mucus covering body. Fins folded, loss of appetite. Fish may lie on its side. Most obvious on dark-coloured fish — *Chilodonelliasis.*
Pale gills with signs of rotting. Breathing rate much increased. Loss of appetite — **Gill rot.**
Cottonwool-like tufts at mouth and on gills. Swollen — or rot-

ting lips. Loss of appetite. Sluggish movements — **Mouth Fungus.**
Open sores on body — Ulcers.

COMPLAINTS

Fungus. Generally, this complaint arises when the fish has been wounded, weakened by parasites, or kept in bad conditions. The fungus spores are present in most still waters, but do not infect healthy fish. The threads of the fungus grow into the skin like roots. Remedy the conditions which have caused the infection. Treat the fish by placing in a saline bath, as follows: Dissolve 1 ounce (28.35 grams) of marine salt, rock salt or cooking salt in each gallon (4.55 litres) of water, and mix well. Do not use table salt, because it contains additives which are harmful to fish. On the second day remove fifty per cent of the solution and replace with a saline solution of double the strength of the first bath. On the third day, again remove fifty per cent of the bath and replace with a similar strength solution to that of the previous day. The fish may remain in this bath until cured, after which the strength of the bath is gradually weakened by removing half of the solution and replacing with freshwater over a period of days.

Cataracts. It may be possible to cure this problem by gently brushing the eye with a solution of iodine which has been diluted by the addition of fifty percent of water — to this add nine parts of glycerine. Mix well by shaking thoroughly.

Argulus. Commonly known as the **Fish louse,** this creature can be introduced when feeding *Daphnia* to the fish if the food is obtained from a wild source. It is a largish, round, flatish creature armed with two suckers and eight legs. It attaches itself, by means of the suckers, to the fish and pushes a "sting" under a scale, to feed upon the blood of its host. Being a large creature, it can be rubbed off — hold the fish in a wet net to carry out this operation. Treat the wound with the iodine solution recommended for the previous complaint.

Flukes. These parasites infest both the gills and the body of the fish, but are too small to be easily seen with the naked eye. In order to eradicate this pest it is necessary to repeat treatment over a period of days. One of the better commercial preparations is 'Sterazin', which can be obtained from aquatic nurseries and the larger dealers in pet fish. An alternative is to use ammonia at the rate of 23 cubic centimetres per gallon (4.55 litres) of water. The ammonia should first be made into a solution of 10 parts of commercial ammonia (by volume) to 90 parts of water. The fish are bathed in the bath from five to twenty minutes, depending upon the tolerance of the fish. It must then be immediately taken out, and placed into fresh water. It may be advisable to repeat the treatment every other day, for four days.

Air Embolism. This complaint is due to an excessive amount of oxygen in the water. In a heavily planted pool with a strong growth of algae, in direct sunlight during a hot day, the vegetation may produce an over-abundance of oxygen. The oxygen-saturated water can cause over-saturation in the blood of the fish. The symptons are air-bubbles in the fins of the fish. Cure by gradually exchanging at least fifty percent of the pool water with clean, cool fresh water.

Fin Rot. An aptly named complaint — a serious disease which may be accompanied by a fungus infection. It is a bacterial infection often caused by chilling or dirty conditions. Treatment may be by means of the saline baths as used against fungus. Another, perhaps better, remedy, is to use Phenoxethol. Make a stock solution by mixing 1 cc of Phenoxethol into each 9 cc of water. The medicinal bath consists of 90 cubic centimetres of the stock solution well stirred into each gallon (4.55 litres) of water. The afflicted fish can remain in the bath until cured.

Leech. If care is not taken this creature can be introduced with plants and other material collected from the wild. It is somewhat worm-like, with sucking discs — one at each end of its body — the front sucking disc surrounding the mouth. Eggs are laid in cocoons on water plants and stones. Place the affected fish in a salt bath for around 15 minutes — this should paralyse the leech and cause it to loosen its grip on the fish. Any which do not leave the fish can be picked off. Be sure to kill the leech by dropping it into boiling water. The only cure for a leech infested pool is to allow it to reman quite dry for a minimum of several weeks.

Chilodonelliasis. This disease can remain latent, striking when resistance is lowered. Although it sometimes attacks pool fish, it is more common in fish kept in aquariums. It is characterised by a thin, grey film of slimy secretion which covers the skin and makes the colours of the fish appear pale. The saline bath, as recommended for fungus, will prove beneficial.

Gill Rot. Highly dangerous, this disease is most prevalent during the summer months. The problem is caused by some of the lower fungi which produce branched hyphae that grow into the veins of the gill sheets. This results in a stoppage of the blood circulation in the affected areas. Due to the lack of a blood supply, sections of the gill sheets die, decay and fall off. The fish usually dies from suffocation. By the time that the symptoms have become obvious it will be too late to save the fish. If the disease is suspected, try the saline baths described for fungus.

Mouth Fungus. This is not a fungus infection, but is caused by a slime bacterium. It is both contagious and dangerous. Infected fish lose their appetite. Movements are sluggish. If treatment is delayed the whole frontal part of the head may be eaten away, and the fish will die. Treat with Phenoxethol as recommended for fin rot.

Ulcers. Often, unless the fish is very special, it is better to destroy any fish that is suffering from ulcers. However, provided the disease is not too advanced, treatment with Phenoxethol may help alleviate the problem.

Lernea. This parasite is commonly known as "anchor worm" and is so-called because of its anchor-shaped front end. This creature buries it head in the body of the fish, leaving its thread-like body exposed. To rid the fish of this parasite it must be held in a wet net, and the creature touched with a very strong solution of potassium permanganate. This is made by dissolving crystals of this chemical in warm water to produce a deep claret colour. This should kill the parasite and allow it to be removed. Treat the wound with a touch of iodine. All fish should be removed from infected waters — this will deprive the parasites of a host and, after two months, they will have died. After this period it should be safe to return the fish.

Ichthyophthiriasis. A *protozoan* parasite which penetrates the *epidermis* and causes small whitish blisters to appear. From these small blisters the complaint derives its common title of "white-spot". This is a very infectious malady and all fish in an infected pool should be treated. Prepare a stock solution of 1 gram of methylene blue dissolved in 100 cc of hot water. Use 4 cc of this solution to each gallon (4.55 litres) of water. The fish can be kept in the bath until all spots remain completely absent from the fish for about one week. The treatment is more effective if the bath temperature can be held at around 68°F. (20°C.) If the infected waters are kept free of fish for two months, the parasites will die through lack of a suitable host. There are some excellent commercial remedies available for the eradication of this dangerous parasite.

Dropsy. Due to an accumulation of fluid within the tissues, the body swells greatly, forcing the scales to stand out instead of lying flat, This problem is difficult to cure, and it is probably much kinder to destroy the ailing fish.

Disorders of the swim-bladder. Try raising the water temperature slightly, and withhold food for a few days, placing a teaspoonful of Epsom salts — to each gallon (4.55 litres) of water — this may help. If the problem was due to constipation, this treatment may bring relief. However, if there is no improvement the fish should be destroyed.

In all cases, the fish should be removed to a special treatment container. A careful watch should also be kept on all stock which has shared the same water, in case they have been infected. The treatments recommended are not always infallible, and all fish must be closely observed when placed into a treatment bath. Some are less tolerant of the medicants or strengths of the bath and, if a fish becomes distressed, it should be immediately removed and the strength of the bath diluted. Care must always be taken to ensure that the fish is not subjected to too great a difference in water temperatures.

Generally, it will be easier to obtain one of the excellent commercial remedies for the specific complaint, rather than buying and mixing the various medicants, and most commercial preparations are relatively cheap and reliable. Some can be used in situ, thus avoiding the need to remove the fish from the pool.

PAINLESS DESTRUCTION

When it is necessary, for whatever reason, to destroy a fish, it should cause no pain. The best way to destroy a fish, if it is large enough, is to grip the tail in a dry cloth and then, very deliberately, knock the back of its head on a hard surface, with a hard, sharp blow. Provided the blow is delivered with determination, death with be instantaneous. Small fish should be firmly dashed against a solid surface. Another method is to drop the fish quickly into very hot boiling water. This will kill the fish instantly. Whichever method is used, it should be executed with firmness — it is far better to use too much force, rather than making the blow in a half-heated manner that is ineffective.

FEEDING

The frequency and amount of feeding is dependent upon a number of factors; not least of these is the quality and temperature of the water. Coldwater fish will have little appetite if the water is becoming polluted or the amount of dissolved oxygen is low. Their appetite will also diminish as the temperature falls, until, at around 40°F. (4.4°C.), the fish will cease to accept food. Therefore gauging the amount and frequency, when feeding, becomes a matter of practice and experience. However, observation will act as a safe guide.

Few fish have died from underfeeding although, if prolonged, it may tend to retard the rate of growth. There is, however, a danger in overfeeding, not because the fish will eat too much, but because of the risk of the uneaten food causing the water to become polluted. Of course, certain live foods do not present this problem.

In the wild, fish have periods of plentiful feeding and periods when food is in short supply. The wise water gardener will endeavour to follow nature in the feeding arrangements, and will recognise that there are times to feed and times to withhold food. In general, when the temperatures are warm and the fish are active, they will feed. When temperatures are cool and the fish show little activity, they will not be inclined to take food.

FOODS

The fish that were discussed in Chapter 6 are all omnivorous in their feeding habits, which is another way of saying that there is very little in the way of food that will not be eaten. Live foods, fresh, frozen or dried animal and vegetable matter, are all readily accepted; indeed, the diet should be as varied as possible. No matter how good a food may be thought or claimed to be, it is a mistake not to make use of alternative foods (we humans would find that even our favourite food would cease to attract and our appetite would dull if we were fed nothing but that one, favourite meal for days on end without variation). It is also recommended that, when possible, feeding should be at regular times. In general wild fish do most of their feeding between the hours of 5 a.m. and 10 p.m. Possibly the best time to feed the fish is first thing in the morning, with a second feed (if thought necessary) a few hours before the sun goes down.

One of the best foods for captive fish is, with little doubt, the earthworm. It is available at most times of the year, no fish refuses it, it carries no water-borne diseases or parasites, and is mildly laxative and easily cleaned. Pink and red worms, such as those found on lawns, are the best, but they should not be gathered from any area which has been treated with any form of chemical preparation. Avoid worms from heavily fertilized land or manure heaps, which excude a yellow secretion and have red rings round their bodies. Small worms can be given whole. Large worms should be chopped into suitable size and given a quick swill under a tap before being thrown into the pool.

Alternatives to the earthworm can be: scraped, lean raw meat, chopped heart or liver, shredded sea-fish (boiled or raw) and chopped fresh shell-fish. Tinned dog and cat foods are also quite useful alternatives. Scrambled egg and oatmeal (as porridge or dry) are good. Live *daphinia,* as sold by pet-fish dealers, together with freeze-dried *daphinia* and other forms of freeze-dried fish foods, may all be offered with confidence. The small maggots sold by anglers supply shops will be accepted, as will the various life-forms that are often found in water butts. Soft green peas, cornflakes, wheat-germ flakes, wholemeal bread and so on can all find a place in the diet of the fish. Modern commercially prepared, dried foods in the form of flakes or pellets, are excellent. Such foods as dried ant's eggs, however, are worthless. On the other hand, the fresh *pupae* taken from an ant nest are very good.

The size of the food should be graded to suit the size of the fish, because if the food is too small the fish will ignore it, and if too large they will not be able to eat it or will choke themselves trying to do so.

The way to keep fish healthy, and promote their sturdy growth, has much to do with a varied diet, the quality of the food, and the correct frequency of feeding, in the proper quantity. Those who care to look, and experiment will find that the spring and summer weather provides an abundance of live foods acceptable to the fish. In the autumn and winter it is not so easy to find a supply of live foods, but there are alternatives, often to be found in the kitchen. The caring fish-owner will usually be willing to go to some trouble to ensure that the fish are provided with a good, nourishing and varied diet to maintain them, not only in good health, but in the very best of condition.

INDEX

Page numbers in italics refer to illustrations

A

Crucian carp (*Carassius carassius*) *68*, 70
Cyprinidae see Carp

D
Daphnia 128, 133
Design of garden 7-8, 11-12, 16, 36
   scale drawing 7-8
Dianthus 81
Diseases of fish 55, 66, 72
   symptoms 123-4, 127-8
   types and treatment 125-6, 128-31
Double digging *see* Trenching
Dragonfly larva 121
Drainage 31
   lawns 92-3
   paths 94, 95, *96*, 97
Dropsy 127, 130
Dry walling 78
Dytiscus 121

E
Earthworms as fish food 132-3
Edelweiss (*Leontopodium*) 81
Electricity use in garden 105ff
   dangers of 105-6
   heaters 113, 120
   illumination 110, 112
   pumps 108-10
   time switches 107
   transformer 107-8
   UK regulations 106
Elodea cadensis 60
E. densa 60
Erica 82, 85ff
E. carnea 82, 86
E. darleyensis 86
E. mediterranea 86
E. terminalis 82
   see also Heather
Erodium 81

F
Fencing 100, 102

Great diving   beetle (*Dytiscus*) 121
Green tench (*Tinca tinca*) 71-2
Gypsophilia 81

H
Hawthorn, water (*Aponogeton distachyus*) 8, 23, 60
Heather 5, 16, 87
    garden 85-6
    see also Erica
Hedges 25, 102
Helianthemum 81
Herbacious border 25
Holly 7, 25
Hornwort (*Ceratophyllum demersum*) 60-1
Hottonia palustris 54, 61
Houseleek (*Sempervivum*) 84
Humus 4, 5, 85

I
Iberis 81
Ichthyophthiriasis (White spot) 127, 130
Illumination 110, 112
    types of lighting 112
    see also Electricity - use in the garden
Informal garden 8, 12, 16, *20, 21, 28*, 29, *30*, 32, 33, 43
    features 11
Insect pests 117
Insecticides 55, 117
Iris kaempferi 62
I. laevigata 62
I. pseudacorus 58, 62, 63
I. versicolour 62

J
Juncus effusus spiralis 62

K
Kabshia section *see* Saxifraga
Koi carp (*Cyprinus carpio var*) 35, 44, *68*, 70-1
    Kohaku 71
    Shusui 71
L
Laburnum 7, 25

Moraine garden *21*
  construction 76ff
Moss control 92
Mossy section *see* Saxifraga
Mouth fungus 128, 130
Myosotis scorpioides 63
Myriophyllum spicatum 61
M. verticillatum 61

N
Navelwort (*Omphalodes*) 83
Newt 121
Nitrogen 5
Numphar lutea 58
Nymphaea a56ff
N. Alba 57, 59
N. Attraction 57
N. Caerulea 56
N. Escarboucle 59
N. Esmerelda 59
N. Froebelli 59
N. Galdstonia 59
N. Graziella 59
N. James Brydon 59
N. Laydekeri lilacea 59
N. Lotus 56
N. x Marliacea albida 59
N. x M. chromatella 59
N. x M. rosea 57
N. odorata sulphurea grandiflora 59
N. Pygmaea helvola 59
N. Rose Arey 59
N. Sultan 59
N. Sunrise 59
N. Tuberosa Richardsonii 59 *see also* Water lilies
Nymphula 117
O
Omphalodes 80, 83
Orfe (*Idus idus*) *68*, 71
Overflow outlet 43
  fountain 29
  water circulation 31
Oxalis 83
Oxygen exhaustion in fish 118-9
P
Pagoda 100
PAR (Parabolic aluminised reflector) 112

Parasites (of fish) 123, 124, 125, 128, 129, 130
Pasque flower (*Pulsatilla*) 83
Paths 3, 16
   construction 14, 94-5
   in marsh areas 32
Patio 12, 95-7, 98, 104, 110
Paving 25, *26*, 94-5, *96*, 97
   construction 97
   patio 95, 97
   patterns *96*
Paxton, Joseph 57
Peat 4, 85
Penstemon 83
P. pinifolius 83
Perch (*Perca fluviatilis*) 72
Pergola 12, *19, 26, 99, 101,* 102, 98-100
Phenoxethol 129, 130
Phlox 83
Phosphates 5
Physa 121
Pickerel weed (*Pontedaria cardata*) 63
Pike *(Esox lucious*) 72
Pipework, plastic 53, 94, *96*
   filters 45, 46
   installation 29, 43
   water circulation 31
   waterfall *48*, 49
Plant containers 25, *34*, 36, 55, 60, 104, 116
Plant foods 5
Plantain, great water 63
Plastic liners 37, *40, 50, 52*
   butyl 41, 47
   polythene 41, 49
   pool construction 41-2, 44
   PVC 41
Plumbing 43 *see also* Pipework
Pollution of water 118, 120, 125
Polygonum 83
Polythene – pool liner 41
   waterfall liner 49
Pond *see* Pool
Pond snail (*Lymnaea*) 121
Pontederia cardata 63
Pool 8, *10, 13,* 16, *18, 20, 21,* 30, *34*
   construction 36-7, *40*, 41-3
   dimensions 35
   filling 51, 116

Saponaria 83
Saururus cernuus 63
Saxifraga 82, 83-4
S. umbrosa 82
Scale drawing 7-8 11-12
Scarification of lawn 92-3
Scirpus albescens 63
S. cernus 63
S. lacustris 63
Screens 14, *15,* 102
   conifers 87
Sedum 82, 84
S. spectabile 82
Sempervivum 84
Shamrock (*Oxalis*) 83
Shelves in pool *34,* 36, 37
Shubunkin (*Carassius auratus var*) *68,* 69
Shusui *see* Koi
Site preparation 1-5
Snails 55, 56, 73, 120-1
Soapwort (*Saponaria*) 83
Soil types 4-5
Spacers in pool construction 38
Spade, correct use 2-3
Statuary 25, 47, 102, *103, 104*
Stepping stones *20,* 32, 33
Steps *17, 20*
   construction 14
'Sterazin' 73, 128
Stone paving 97
Stonecrop (*Sedum*) 84
Stream 14, *21,* 29, 42, *52*
   diversion of 51
Submersible pump 27, 108, *109,* 110
Surface pump 108, *111*
   housing 110
Swamp lily (*Saururus carnuus*) 63
Sweet flag (*Acorus calamus*) 62
Swim-bladder disorders 124, 127, 130-1

T
Tadpole 121
Taj Mahal 25
Tench (*Tinca tinca*) *68,* 71-2
Terrace 104
Thymus 84
Time switches 107